AIR-FRYER
COOKBOOK

365 DAYS OF QUICK & EASY RECIPES FOR HEALTHY COOKING WITH YOUR AIR FRYER

BY FINLEY MACK

© Copyright 2021 by - Finley Mack - All rights reserved.

This document is geared towards providing exact and reliable information in regards to the topic and issue covered. The publication is sold with the idea that the publisher is not required to render accounting, officially permitted, or otherwise, qualified services. If advice is necessary, legal or professional, a practiced individual in the profession should be ordered.

- From a Declaration of Principles which was accepted and approved equally by a Committee of the American Bar Association and a Committee of Publishers and Associations.

In no way is it legal to reproduce, duplicate, or transmit any part of this document in either electronic means or in printed format. Recording of this publication is strictly prohibited and any storage of this document is not allowed unless with written permission from the publisher. All rights reserved.

The information provided herein is stated to be truthful and consistent, in that any liability, in terms of inattention or otherwise, by any usage or abuse of any policies, processes, or directions contained within is the solitary and utter responsibility of the recipient reader. Under no reparation, damages, or monetary loss due to the information herein, either directly or indirectly.

All data and information provided in this book is for informational purposes only. Finley Mack makes no representations as to accuracy, completeness, current, suitability, or validity of any information in this book & will not be liable for any errors, omissions, or delays in this information or any losses, injuries, or damages arising from its display or use. All information is provided on an as-is basis. Respective authors own all copyrights not held by the publisher.

The information herein is offered for informational purposes solely, and is universal as so. The presentation of the information is without contract or any type of guarantee assurance.

The trademarks that are used are without any consent, and the publication of the trademark is without permission or backing by the trademark owner. All trademarks and brands within this book are for clarifying purposes only and are owned by the owners themselves, not affiliated with this document.

The author is not a licensed practitioner, physician or medical professional and offers no medical treatment, diagnoses, suggestions or counselling. The information presented herein has not been evaluated by the U.S Food & Drug Administration, and it is not intended to diagnose, treat, cure or prevent any disease. Full medical clearance from a licensed physician should be obtained before beginning or modifying any diet, exercise or lifestyle program, and physician should be informed of all nutritional changes. The author claims no responsibility to any person or entity for any liability, loss, damage or death caused or alleged to be caused directly or indirectly as a result of the use, application or interpretation of the information presented herein.

TABLE OF CONTENTS

INTRODUCTION 5
Fried foods are bad for your health. 7
The health benefits of using
an air fryer to cook food 7
The taste and crunch of
fried food without the oil. 8
Tips for air fryer success 9
Cooking times and temperatures
for commonly eaten foods. 10
Things your air fryer can't do. 11

BREAKFASTS 13
Banana Quinoa. 14
Pecan Banana Loaf 15
Cranberry & Nut Bar. 16
Apple Chicken Patties 17
Coconut Doughnuts. 18
Vegetable Hash. 19
Berry Bread Casserole 20
Sirloin & Eggs 21
Double Choco Cupcakes 22
Crust-less Quiche 23
Spinach Wraps 24
Zucchini Loaf. 25
Cinnamon Buns 26
Red Pepper Hash 28
Blueberry Buns. 29

SNACKS & APPETIZERS 30
Lemon Garbanzo Beans 31
Asian Chicken Skewers. 32
Shrimp Wonton 33
Dried Tofu 34
Dill Pickle Chips. 35
Stuffed Peppers 36
Pepper Popcorn 37

Mediterranean Meatballs 38
Sweet Potato Chips. 39
Broccoli Dip 40
Garlic Potato Wedges 41
Italian Rice Balls 42
Cheesy Bacon Sticks 43
Mini Beef Burgers 44

FISH & SEAFOOD 45
Spicy Salmon. 46
Mint & Lime Haddock. 47
Orange Halibut. 48
Lime Trout 49
Cod & Garbanzo Salad 50
Pear Scallops. 51
Sriracha Shrimp Tortillas 52
Potato Cod Cakes. 53
Crumbed Crab 54
Haddock Sandwich. 55
Shrimp Feta Pockets. 56
Smoked Paprika Flounder 57
Harissa Tilapia 58
Cajun-Spiced Catfish 59
Chinese Spice Tuna 60

POULTRY 61
BBQ Chicken & Slaw. 62
Tomato Turkey Balls 63
Asian Spicy Wings 64
Serrano Chicken Wraps 65
Cayenne Turkey Breasts 66
Cheesy Chicken Buns. 67
Turkey Sausage Roast. 68
Chicken Schnitzel. 69
Italian Chicken Cutlets 70
Peach-Coated Drumsticks 71

Turkey Pops 72
Marinara Chicken Balls. 73
Sweet Chicken Skewers 74
Herbed Hen Roast 75
Chicken Parmesan 76

BEEF, LAMB, & PORK.....................77

Dijon Roast Pork 78
Honey & Mustard Chops. 79
Rosemary Beef Roast. 80
Honey Hickory Ribs. 81
Tzatziki Pork Pitas 82
Honey NY Strip 83
Hawaiian Beef Sandwich 84
Japanese Miso Steak 85
Cumin Lamb Chops. 86
Sausage-Stuffed Peppers 87
Beef Stew Fry. 88
Chinese Pork Chops. 89
Ground Beef Loaf 90
Mediterranean Lamb Ovals 91
Vegetable & Pork Skewers 92

VEGETARIAN MAINS 93

Roasted Carrots with Nuts. 94
Legume Burgers 95
Garbanzo Fritters. 96
Spanish Rice 97
Stuffed Eggplant 98
Garbanzo Bean Tortillas 99
Crumbed Tomatoes 100
Tomato Rotini. 101
Black Bean Patties 102
Shiitake Quinoa 103
Mediterranean Eggplant 104
Tofu Curry 105
Kale Pizza. 106
Sambal Brussels Sprouts 107
BBQ Broccoli Bites 108

SIDES 109

Mozzarella Potato Bake 110
Feta Sweet Potato. 111
Romano Broccoli Dip 112
Mexican Stuffed Poblano. 113
Greek Rice Balls. 115
Lemon & Lime Fennel. 116
Zucchini Fries. 117
Garbanzo Turkey Salad 118
Orange Zucchinis 119
Herb Eggplant Salad 120
Tortilla Crisps 121
Balsamic Green Pepper 122
Chili & Lime Corn 123
Savory Dinner Rolls 124
Crumbed Avo. 125
Coriander Parsnips. 126

DESSERTS 127

Strawberry Pie. 128
Peaches & Cream 129
Cinnamon Cake Bites. 130
Date Choco Cookies 131
Sweet Potato Wraps 132
Caramel Apples. 133
Caramel Banana Pastry. 134
Chocolate Slices 135
Berry Ganache Cake. 136
Citrus Slices 137
Carrot Cupcakes. 138
Blueberry Shortcake 139
Molten Chocolate Cake 140
Pecan & Pear Bake 141
Apple Pies. 142

METRIC EQUIVALENCE CHART 143

Metric Equivalence Chart 144

INTRODUCTION

The mere mention of fried food can make a person's mouth water. Crispy fried chicken, French fries, doughnuts, crumbed fish, samosas. Just reading the words can make you want to run out to your favorite fast food outlet.

For decades, weight and health issues have been linked to eating too much fatty food. If you can't manage to tear yourself away from your oily fried food obsession, you may be struggling to maintain a healthy weight, and your doctor may have told you to start keeping an eye on your cholesterol and blood sugar levels.

People don't just eat to fuel their bodies. A lot of us eat because we just love the taste of food. We love the crunchy texture of food cooked in boiling hot oil. We dig in, even though we know it is not good for us. It is the ultimate comfort food. If only there was a way to enjoy all of our favorite crispy-on-the-outside, fluffy-on-the-inside, scrumptious foods, without feeling guilty about making ourselves fat and sick.

Enter the air fryer! It is the answer to all of our comfort food prayers. Delicious fried food, without the fat and the guilt. It offers you a revolutionary new way to cook almost anything with very little oil. And it is super quick and easy.

I have always been very cautious about the amounts and types of fats I use in cooking. I am all too aware of the consequences of eating an unhealthy diet. Every now and then, I will treat my family to a good old fry-up. And they always ask for more!

My mom always had a chip pot on the stove, full of oil that she used to make chips for supper, at least three times per week. I am not sure how often the oil was changed, but it wasn't as regularly as it should have been. Her chips were always great, though. I can't bring myself to do that, even with clean oil, every time I deep fry anything.

I had my eye on an air fryer for a long time. I went backwards and forwards, wanting one more than anything, and then talking myself out of it, asking myself when I would use it. Turns out, now that I have one (yes, I finally gave in to my desire), I use it all the time!

Like all busy moms, I am juggling all the balls: lunchboxes, the school run, work, extra murals, and, of course, cooking dinner every night. If only I had known sooner how much easier the air fryer would make getting dinner on the table. And I no longer feel guilty about serving up some crispy, steaming French fries.

On the odd occasion when it is just me and my husband at home, or it's just me for dinner, I can pop something in the air fryer, and have something delicious to eat in almost no time at all.

Now that I know how wonderful the air fryer is, I am constantly wondering what I can cook in it. The recipes in this book offer a wonderful variety of quick, healthy meals. Did you know that your air fryer can successfully cook everything from eggs to fritters to muffins; zucchini fries to chicken wings to meatballs; roasted peppers to potatoes to green beans; fish to chicken to steak?

I hope you enjoy cooking with your air fryer as much as I enjoy cooking with mine.

FRIED FOODS ARE BAD FOR YOUR HEALTH

Frying food normally involves some kind of fat; usually vegetable oil. It is heated to a temperature that is around twice that of boiling point. Very hot oil is important, to prevent too much oil being absorbed into the food you are cooking.

Your choice of oil adds a distinctive flavor to your fried food. Commonly used oils are sunflower oil, canola oil, olive oil, peanut oil, and sesame oil.

The oil is just part of the flavor profile of fried foods, though. Most of the irresistible flavor comes from what the heat does to the crumbs or batter that coats the food. The starches in the coating are caramelized, making them slightly sweeter, and more digestible - and don't forget, crunchy.

The combination of the high cooking temperature, the oil itself, and the browning reaction on the surface of the food is what gives fried food its distinctive, irresistible crunch and flavor. But the oil is the reason fried food is bad for our health.

While a moderate amount of fat is important for maintaining health, too much, and the wrong kind of fat, is a problem. Fat is a very dense source of calories, and it can be easy to eat too much, especially if you love fried food. This can make maintaining a healthy weight very difficult.

When oil is heated to the temperatures required for frying food, the chemical structure of the oil becomes denatured. These denatured fats and saturated fats, such as those found in cheese, meat, and chicken skin, contribute to raised cholesterol levels. They raise your risk of developing cardiovascular disease.

That is why your doctor or dietitian will always tell you to cut back on fried food. There is strong scientific evidence to support this piece of advice.

THE HEALTH BENEFITS OF USING AN AIR FRYER TO COOK FOOD

Luckily, the clever people who are constantly coming up with new ideas and gadgets for cooking food, invented the air fryer. Now we have a way of cooking our food so that it tastes just like fried food, but with very little fat.

Foods like frozen battered fish, chicken schnitzel, and baked potatoes can be cooked in the air fryer, without adding any additional oil. You may want to mix a little oil with your sweet potato fries, or brush your steak with some oil before cooking it. The amount you need is significantly less than you would use in a deep fryer. All you need is a teaspoon full. This simple fact makes cooking in the air fryer a healthier option.

THE TASTE AND CRUNCH OF FRIED FOOD WITHOUT THE OIL

You may be wondering how it is possible to cook food without oil, and still get all the crunch and tastiness? This countertop convection oven has a heated coil at the top, and a fan that moves the heated air around the food that you place in a mesh basket.

The method of frying results in the surface of the food dehydrating. This is part of the reason it becomes crispy and browned. Normally, cooking food in a convection oven creates steam, which is not conducive to crunchiness and browning. When you add the fan, the steam is removed from the surface of the food, and the hot temperature cooks the outside of the food just as quickly as it would be cooked in a deep fryer.

Healthy fried foods are not the only benefit of using an air fryer. The table below lists some of the other benefits of an air fryer.

Benefit	
Less or no oil	There are many reasons why this is a good thing. Firstly, you don't have to waste time and electricity heating up a lot of oil to fry your food. Secondly, it is a great way to eat crunchy, delicious food, without having a negative impact on your health.
Uses less energy	With the cost of electricity forever climbing, it makes sense to use a kitchen appliance that uses less than your oven or stove. Only a small space is being heated, and the cooking times are faster.
Less mess	Only the basket you cook your food in needs to be cleaned. Your stove and countertops are spared the oil splatter.
Portable	Even the bigger air fryers are small enough for you to take with you when you go on a self-catering vacation.
Easy to use	No big, clumsy oven trays, or complicated settings.
Faster cooking	The high temperatures, combined with the fan, reduce your cooking time.
Quick meals for kids	Hungry kids are grumpy kids. Your air fryer means that your children can enjoy the foods they love best, in almost no time at all.
Convenient meals for one or two people	Cooking for yourself can be a bit of a drag. Even cooking for two can feel like a waste of time. When your time spent in the kitchen preparing meals is cut down, and the food you serve is delicious, it is no longer a chore to cook for just one or two people.

Consistent results	Because the temperature is set at the beginning of the cooking process, and the cooking times in the air fryer have been so well tested, you will get the same result every time you cook.
No pre-heating	Only a small space needs to be heated by the powerful element and fan. That means that you do not have to preheat your air fryer. It gets up to the required temperature very quickly.
Perfect portions	When you cook in a large oven, or you are heating up a lot of oil, you may feel like you need to fill the space with whatever you are cooking. How often do you have leftovers? Due to the smaller size, it is easier to cook just the right amount, without worrying about all the wasted space.

TIPS FOR AIR FRYER SUCCESS

Using the air fryer is as easy as 1,2,3. Air fryers come in different shapes and sizes, but they all do the same thing. It is always a good idea to familiarize yourself with your air fryer by reading the user manual. It will save you the frustration of trying to figure it out when you have a hungry family to feed.

You can fry, roast, grill, or bake in your air fryer. It isn't exclusively reserved for making French fries!

Use these tips to make sure you have perfectly cooked, crunchy, scrumptious food every time:

1. Preheat your air fryer if your model requires that it is hot before you put the food into it.
2. Place your food in the air fryer drawer or basket. It should not be more than ⅔ full.
3. Insert the filled drawer or basket.
4. Select your temperature.
5. Set the timer for the desired cooking time. (If your air fryer does not need to be preheated, you can add three minutes to your cooking time instead.)
6. Check the food half way through the cooking time. Remove it from the air fryer, and shake it or move it around, to ensure even cooking.
7. Adjust the temperature, if necessary.
8. Once cooking is complete, remove the drawer or basket from the air fryer, and place it on a heat resistant surface.

There are many ways to make your air fryer the most used appliance in your kitchen.

#1 Invest in some accessories

Accessories are not essential for the everyday use of your air fryer, but they can open up some exciting cooking possibilities. An oven-safe baking dish or cake pan, that fits into your air fryer without touching the sides, means you can cook foods that start off as a liquid. Mini foil pie pans and cupcake liners are also useful.

#2 Adapt your traditional recipes with ease

You are not restricted to cooking food from recipes that have been created specifically for the air fryer. You can easily adapt your old recipes for perfect results in your new favorite appliance. Simply reduce the cooking temperature by 50°F (10°C), and halve your cooking time.

#3 Boost the browning

Most foods need a little help to brown to perfection. That is why some oil is called for in most recipes. Using an oil spray is a handy way of coating the surface of the food with just a little oil. Glazes also add great color to your food, and extra flavor, especially if they contain ingredients like honey, hoisin sauce, or chutney.

#4 Add water to prevent drying

A bit of dehydration on the surface of most of the foods you cook in your air fryer will give you the results you are looking for - brown, crispy food. But some foods, such as vegetables, can dry out a bit too much. To make sure your veggies come out of the air fryer cooked to perfection, add a little water in the bottom of the cooking drawer or basket. That will create a steam-roasting effect, that is a winning strategy for cooking foods that contain a lot of moisture.

#5 Consider using skewers

When your meat, fish, or chicken is cut into smaller chunks, and slipped onto a skewer, more of your meat is exposed to the hot air in the air fryer. Your meat will have more flavor and texture than if you cooked it whole.

#6 Flip your food half way

The heat in an air fryer only comes from the top of the oven. For better cooking results, it is a good idea to flip your food over half way through cooking, so that it browns evenly on all sides.

#7 Single layer of food only

Don't be tempted to cook too much food at once. Best results are achieved if there is only a single layer of food in your cooking drawer or basket. That way, all of the food is evenly heated.

COOKING TIMES AND TEMPERATURES FOR COMMONLY EATEN FOODS

You can refer to the recipes for suggested cooking times and temperatures. Listed below are the suggested cooking times and temperatures for foods that are most commonly cooked in the air fryer.

Food	Temperature	Food
Bacon	330°F (165°C)	10 to 12 minutes
Chicken schnitzel	400°F (200°C)	7 to 8 minutes
Chicken wings or drumettes	400°F (200°C)	22 to 24 minutes
Salmon fillet	400°F (200°C)	7 minutes
Pork steak	400°F (200°C)	8 minutes
Beef steak	400°F (200°C)	10 minutes
Asparagus	380°F (190°C)	8 to 10 minutes
Baked potato	400°F (200°C)	35 minutes
French fries	380°F (190°C)	12 minutes

THINGS YOUR AIR FRYER CAN'T DO

The air fryer may seem like the miracle appliance that makes cooking for yourself and your family a breeze. While there is a lot it can do very well, it doesn't do everything well. For one thing, it is not self-cleaning!

Jokes aside, there are some meals your stove top or slow cooker would be more suited to.

Cook in the air fryer	Don't cook in the air fryer
- Potatoes - Squash - Peppers - Roasted carrots - Broccoli - Cauliflower - Meat suitable for frying or roasting - Fish - Chicken - Frozen crumbed foods such as fish, or chicken schnitzel - Lasagna - Cakes - Cookies - Muffins	- Soups - Sauces - Pasta - Foods that are coated in a wet batter without being dipped in bread crumbs - Meat suitable for stews

As you can see, the list of foods that can be successfully cooked in the air fryer is longer than the list of those that are not suitable. Some foods have a better taste and texture if they are cooked at lower temperatures for longer.

How to clean your air fryer

Unfortunately, the air fryer is not all fun and games. It does need to be cleaned after you use it. Luckily, even though you are making all of your favorite fried foods, there is a lot less oily residue to clean up afterwards. The air fryer is as easy to clean as it is to use.

First, some important notes about cleaning your air fryer:

1. It is an electrical appliance, so whatever you do, don't submerge it in water.
2. Be gentle with it. Avoid using metal utensils, and abrasive sponges or wire brushes to remove cooked food particles. You don't want to damage the non-stick coating in your air fryer.
3. To remove any foul odors, you can simply place half a lemon inside the air fryer for half an hour before you clean it.

The food basket or drawer should be washed with warm soapy water and a soft sponge, after every use. It is also a good idea to wipe the inside of the air fryer with a damp sponge. Make sure to dry the surfaces once they are clean.

Are you ready to cook up a storm?

The air fryer is a truly wonderful invention. Cooking healthy food has never been easier. The best part is, you can eat healthy without compromising on your favorite tastes. Crispy fried chicken, French fries, and doughnuts can be enjoyed more often - completely guilt-free.

The recipes in this book highlight the versatility of the air fryer. Whether you would normally be frying, baking, roasting, or grilling, the air fryer can produce meals that are at least as tasty as the original product, sometimes even better because they are less oily.

Less oil means more health. Say goodbye to artery-clogging deep fried food. It is a convenient way to make sure you consume less fat in your diet, especially denatured, overheated oils that can raise your cholesterol levels, and cause chronic inflammation, which has been linked to numerous health conditions.

Not only is it better for your health, but you will be consuming fewer calories. Using an air fryer to fry your food makes watching your weight a lot easier. You don't have to say no to all of your favorite foods. All foods truly do fit when you don't have to worry about excess oils and calories.

Put on your apron, and plug in your air fryer. Page through the recipes, and decide what you are having for dinner tonight. If you are cooking for yourself, you and your partner, or the whole family, the air fryer will make sure that dinner is on the table in half an hour.

No mess, no fuss. Quick, easy, tasty meals, and an easy cleanup. What more could a busy mom, businessman, or unenthusiastic cook want? Breakfast, lunch, dinner, or a tasty baked treat. The wonderful world of air frying is at your fingertips.

BREAKFASTS

BREAKFASTS

BANANA QUINOA

COOK TIME: 1 HOUR | SERVES: 1

Ingredients:

- 5 tbsp quinoa
- 1¼ cups boiling water
- ⅛ tsp vanilla extract
- ⅛ tbsp fine salt
- 2–4 tbsp whole milk
- 1 tbsp olive oil
- 1½ tsp honey, plus extra for drizzling
- 1 small banana, chopped

Directions:

1. Preheat the air fryer to 400°F, or 200°C.

2. Place the quinoa in a medium-sized oven proof bowl, and cover with cold water. Allow to soak at room temperature for 8 to 24 hours. Drain, and rinse well.

3. To the same bowl with the drained and rinsed quinoa, add the boiling water, vanilla extract, and fine salt. Cover tightly with aluminum foil.

4. Put the bowl in the air-fryer basket, and place it into the air fryer. Cook for 45 minutes, until the quinoa is tender, and beginning to burst.

5. Carefully remove the basket from the air fryer. Mix 2 tbsp whole milk, the olive oil, and the honey into the porridge, and allow to sit, uncovered, for 5 minutes. The porridge will thicken as it sits.

6. Add the remaining 2 tbsp whole milk if needed. Top with chopped bananas, and drizzle with extra honey before serving.

BREAKFASTS

PECAN BANANA LOAF

COOK TIME: 37 MIN | MAKES: 1 LOAF

INGREDIENTS:

- ¾ cup all-purpose flour
- ¼ tsp fine salt
- ¼ tsp baking soda
- 2 large bananas, mashed
- ½ cup granulated sugar
- ¼ cup sunflower oil
- ¼ cup sour cream
- ½ tsp vanilla extract
- 1 large egg
- ½ cup pecan nuts, chopped

DIRECTIONS:

1. Preheat the air fryer to 310°F, or 154°C.

2. In a large mixing bowl, add together the all-purpose flour, fine salt, and baking soda. Whisk to combine, and set aside.

3. In a medium-sized mixing bowl, combine the mashed bananas, granulated sugar, sunflower oil, sour cream, vanilla extract, and large egg. Whisk until completely smooth.

4. Fold the dry ingredients into the wet ingredients until just combined. Don't overmix. Gently fold in the chopped pecan nuts.

5. Pour the batter into a nonstick, 6 to 7-inch loaf pan, and place inside the air fryer basket.

6. Bake for 33 to 37 minutes, or until a toothpick inserted comes out clean.

7. Allow the banana loaf to cool in the pan on a wire rack for 20 minutes, before removing and serving.

BREAKFASTS

CRANBERRY & NUT BAR

COOK TIME: 10 MIN | MAKES: 10 BARS

Ingredients:

- 1 cup honey and oats granola
- ½ cup cashew butter
- ½ cup cashew nuts
- ½ cup dried cranberries
- ½ cup unsweetened coconut flakes
- 4 tbsp honey
- ½ tsp fine salt
- Non-stick cooking spray

Directions:

1. Set the air fryer temperature to 350°F, or 180°C.

2. Add together the honey and oats granola, cashew butter, cashew nuts, dried cranberries, coconut flakes, honey, and fine salt in a food processor, and pulse to combine.

3. Coat a 7-inch (17.5cm) round pan with non-stick cooking spray, and evenly press the mixture into the bottom of the pan, until tightly packed.

4. Place the pan in the fryer basket, and bake for 10 minutes, until the edges begin to brown.

5. Carefully remove the pan from the fryer basket, and allow the granola to cool completely on a wire rack before removing.

6. Remove the cooled granola from the pan, and cut it into 10 bars.

BREAKFASTS

APPLE CHICKEN PATTIES

COOK TIME: 10 MIN | SERVES: 4

Ingredients:

- 1 tbsp sage, chopped
- 1 tbsp parsley, chopped
- 1¼ tsp sea salt
- ¾ tsp smoked paprika
- ½ tsp garlic powder
- ½ tsp onion powder
- ⅛ tsp ground black pepper
- ⅛ tsp crushed red pepper flakes
- 1 lb. ground chicken
- ½ cup Fuji or Gala apples, peeled, and finely minced

Directions:

1. Preheat the air fryer to 400°F, or 200°C.

2. In a medium-sized mixing bowl, add together the chopped sage, chopped parsley, sea salt, smoked paprika, garlic powder, onion powder, ground black pepper, and crushed red pepper flakes. Mix to combine.

3. Add the ground chicken and minced apples to the bowl with the spice mixture, and work the spices into the meat with your hands until well blended. Shape into 8 patties.

4. Working in batches, arrange a single layer of the chicken patties in the air fryer basket.

5. Cook each batch for 10 minutes, flipping half way, until the meat is browned, and fully cooked. Serve warm.

Tip: for a toaster oven–style air fryer, the temperature and timing stay the same.

Cooking tip: place the chicken patties in the fridge for 1 hour, to firm up, before cooking.

BREAKFASTS

COCONUT DOUGHNUTS

COOK TIME: 6 MIN | MAKES: 12

Ingredients:

- 2 tbsp ground flaxseed
- 6 tbsp water
- 1 cup plus 2 tbsp all-purpose flour
- ½ tsp fine salt
- 1 tsp ground cinnamon
- 1 tsp baking powder
- ¼ cup light brown sugar
- ¼ cup unsweetened almond milk
- 1 tbsp coconut oil, melted
- Non-stick cooking spray

Honey syrup coating:
- ¼ cup honey
- ¼ cup warm water
- ½ cup unsweetened desiccated coconut

Directions:

1. Preheat the air fryer to 370°F, or 190°C.

2. In a small mixing bowl, add together the ground flaxseed and water. Mix to combine.

3. In a large mixing bowl, add together the all-purpose flour, fine salt, ground cinnamon, and baking powder. Whisk to combine.

4. Add in the light brown sugar, almond milk, melted coconut oil, and flaxseed mixture. Mix until a sticky dough forms, and place the dough in the fridge for 1 hour.

5. Coat the air fryer basket with nonstick cooking spray.

6. While the air fryer is heating, combine the honey and warm water in a medium-sized mixing bowl, and mix until the honey has dissolved. Set aside. Place the desiccated coconut in another mixing bowl, and set aside.

7. Divide the dough into 12 equal pieces with a small ice cream scoop. Roll the dough into balls.

8. Place the balls in the fryer basket, and cook for 6 minutes, until puffed up and golden brown.

9. Remove the doughnut balls, and place them immediately into the honey-water mixture, and then into the desiccated coconut. Toss to coat.

10. Transfer the doughnut balls onto a platter, and serve immediately.

BREAKFASTS

VEGETABLE HASH

COOK TIME: 18 MIN | SERVES: 6

INGREDIENTS:

- 2 medium butternut squash, peeled, seeded, and cut into cubes
- 1 medium green bell pepper, seeded and diced
- ½ red onion, finely chopped
- 4 oz white mushrooms, diced
- 2 tbsp olive oil
- ½ tbsp garlic, minced
- ½ tsp sea salt
- ½ tsp ground black pepper
- ½ tbsp parsley, chopped
- ½ tsp red pepper flakes

DIRECTIONS:

1. Preheat the air fryer to 380°F, or 200°C.

2. In a large mixing bowl, combine the cubed butternut squash, diced green bell pepper, chopped red onion, diced mushrooms, olive oil, minced garlic, sea salt, ground black pepper, chopped parsley, and red pepper flakes. Toss to coat the vegetables.

3. Place the seasoned vegetables into the air fryer basket, making sure that they are in a single layer.

4. Cook for 18 minutes, tossing the vegetables half way through cooking.

5. Transfer to a serving bowl, and enjoy.

Substitution tip: you can use sweet potato, pumpkin, or Brussels sprouts in place of the butternut squash.

BREAKFASTS

BERRY BREAD CASSEROLE

COOK TIME: 15 MIN | SERVES: 2

Ingredients:

- Non-stick cooking spray
- 4 slices whole grain bread, cubed
- 1 cup frozen whole berry medley
- 1 tbsp ground flaxseed
- 3 tbsp water
- 1 cup whole milk
- 1 tsp vanilla extract
- 2 tbsp honey, plus more for serving
- 1 tbsp orange zest

Directions:

1. Preheat the air fryer to 350°F, or 180°C. Spray a baking dish with nonstick cooking spray.

2. Place the cubed bread and berry medley into the baking dish, and set aside.

3. In a small mixing bowl, add together the ground flaxseed and water, and mix to combine.

4. In a medium-sized mixing bowl, add together the whole milk, vanilla extract, honey, orange zest, and flaxseed mixture. Whisk to combine. Pour the liquid mixture over the bread and berries. Gently press down to submerge the bread.

5. Place the dish in the fryer basket, and bake for 15 minutes, until the edges are golden brown, and the center is firm.

6. Remove the dish from the fryer basket, and allow the casserole to cool for 10 minutes. Serve in bowls, and drizzle with the extra honey.

BREAKFASTS

SIRLOIN & EGGS

COOK TIME: 14 MIN | SERVES: 2

INGREDIENTS:

For the steak:
- Aluminum foil
- 2 (6 oz) sirloin steaks
- 1 tsp garlic, minced
- ¼ tsp fine salt
- ¼ tsp ground black pepper

For the eggs:
- Non-stick cooking spray
- 2 large eggs
- ¼ tsp fine salt
- ¼ tsp ground black pepper
- ¼ tsp smoked paprika
- 1 tsp parsley, chopped

DIRECTIONS:

To make the steak

1. Preheat the air fryer to 360°F, or 180°C.

2. Place the sirloin steaks in the fryer basket. No seasoning at this point.

3. Bake for 5 minutes, flip, and then add the minced garlic, fine salt, and ground pepper. Bake for another 4 minutes.

4. Transfer the sirloin steaks onto a plate, and cover with aluminum foil to keep warm.

To make the eggs

5. Reduce the temperature to 330°F, or 165°C.

6. Coat 2 ramekins with non-stick cooking spray.

7. Crack 1 large egg into each ramekin.

8. Sprinkle fine salt, ground black pepper, smoked paprika, and chopped parsley over each egg.

9. Bake for 5 minutes, until set. Serve warm with the sirloin steaks.

BREAKFASTS

DOUBLE CHOCO CUPCAKES

COOK TIME: 12 MIN | MAKES: 4

Ingredients:

- ½ cup all-purpose flour
- 2 tbsp unsweetened cocoa powder
- ¾ tsp baking powder
- ⅛ tsp fine salt
- ¼ cup granulated sugar
- 3 tbsp sunflower oil
- White of 1 large egg
- 3 tbsp sour cream
- 1 tsp vanilla extract
- ¼ cup dark chocolate chips, plus more for topping

Directions:

1. Preheat the air fryer to 350°F, or 180°C.

2. In a medium-sized mixing bowl, add together the all-purpose flour, unsweetened cocoa powder, baking powder, and fine salt. Mix to combine. Whisk in the granulated sugar and sunflower oil.

3. Add in the egg white, sour cream, and vanilla extract. Don't overmix.

4. Fold in the dark chocolate chips.

5. Divide the batter evenly into 4 oven-proof muffin cups, filling them to about half way.

6. Top with the extra dark chocolate chips.

7. Bake for 12 minutes, or until a toothpick inserted into the middle comes out clean. Serve warm.

CRUST-LESS QUICHE

COOK TIME: 4 MIN | SERVES: 6

Ingredients:

- 4 large eggs
- 2 cups shredded cheddar cheese
- ½ cup plain cottage cheese
- ¼ cup whipping cream
- 1 tbsp bacon pieces
- ½ tsp sea salt
- ½ tsp ground black pepper
- 2 tbsp chives, chopped

Directions:

1. Preheat the air fryer to 360°F, or 180°C.

2. In a blender, combine the large eggs, shredded cheddar cheese, plain cottage cheese, whipping cream, bacon pieces, sea salt, ground black pepper and chopped chives. Blend on high for 20 seconds.

3. Pour the egg mixture into a silicone muffin mold. Place the mold inside the air fryer basket, and bake for 4 minutes, until the quiches are no longer moist on top. Serve warm.

BREAKFASTS

SPINACH WRAPS

COOK TIME: 8 MIN | SERVES: 6

Ingredients:

- 8 large eggs
- ¼ cup whole milk
- ⅛ tsp sea salt
- 2 tbsp olive oil, divided
- 8 oz frozen chopped spinach, thawed and squeezed dry
- 6 spring onions, thinly sliced
- 1½ tsp smoked paprika
- ½ tsp ground cayenne pepper
- 1 (15 oz) can black beans
- ¼ cup parsley, chopped
- 2 tbsp lime juice
- Sea salt
- Ground black pepper
- 6 whole-wheat tortillas

Directions:

1. Preheat the air fryer to 400°F, or 200°C.

2. In a medium-sized mixing bowl, add together the large eggs, whole milk, and sea salt, and whisk to combine.

3. Heat 1 tbsp olive oil in a heavy bottom pan over medium heat until hot. Add the egg mixture, and cook for 2 to 4 minutes, using a rubber spatula to scrape along the bottom and sides of the pan, constantly and firmly, until the eggs are just set. Fold in the chopped spinach. Transfer the egg mixture onto a plate, and wipe the pan clean with paper towels.

4. Heat the remaining 1 tbsp olive oil in the clean pan over medium heat until hot. Add the sliced spring onions, smoked paprika, and ground cayenne pepper, and cook for 1 minute, until fragrant.

5. Mix in the black beans, with their liquid, and cook for 3 to 5 minutes, mashing the beans with the back of a spoon, until the mixture is heated through, and has thickened. Remove from the heat, and mix in the chopped parsley and lime juice. Season with sea salt and ground black pepper to taste.

6. Place the tortilla wraps on a damp dishtowel, and microwave for 1 minute, until warm. Lay the tortillas on the counter, and spread the bean mixture evenly across each one. Top with the egg and spinach mixture.

7. Working with 1 tortilla at a time, fold in the sides, then the bottom of the tortilla, over the filling, then continue to roll tightly into a wrap.

8. Arrange up to 4 wraps, seam side down, in the air-fryer basket, spaced evenly apart. Place the basket into the air fryer, and cook for 5 to 8 minutes, until crisp. Serve warm.

BREAKFASTS

ZUCCHINI LOAF

COOK TIME: 35 MIN | MAKES: 1 LOAF

Ingredients:

- Non-stick cooking spray
- ½ cup all-purpose flour
- ¼ cup unsweetened cocoa powder
- ½ tsp baking soda
- ¼ tsp fine salt
- 1 large egg at room temperature
- 6 tbsp light brown sugar
- 2 tbsp unsalted butter, melted and slightly cooled
- 2 tbsp sunflower oil
- ½ tsp vanilla extract
- ¾ cup shredded zucchinis, patted dry
- ½ cup dark chocolate chips, divided

Directions:

1. Preheat the air fryer to 310°F, or 150°C.

2. Spray a mini loaf pan with non-stick cooking spray, and set aside.

3. In a medium-sized mixing bowl, add together the all-purpose flour, unsweetened cocoa powder, baking soda, and fine salt. Whisk to combine, and set aside.

4. In a large mixing bowl, combine the large egg, light brown sugar, unsalted melted butter, sunflower oil, and vanilla extract. Whisk until smooth.

5. Add the dry ingredients into the wet, and mix until smooth.

6. Fold in the shredded zucchinis, and half of the dark chocolate chips.

7. Pour the batter into the prepared loaf pan, and sprinkle the remaining dark chocolate chips on top. Place the pan inside the air fryer basket.

8. Bake for 30 to 35 minutes, or until a toothpick inserted comes out clean.

9. Remove, and allow to cool for 30 minutes on a wire rack.

10. Remove the bread from the loaf pan, and serve.

BREAKFASTS

CINNAMON BUNS

COOK TIME: 22 MIN | SERVES: 7

Ingredients:

Dough
- 1⅛ tsp active dry yeast
- ¼ cup warm water
- 2 tsp granulated sugar
- 2 tbsp low-fat milk
- 1 large egg
- ¼ tsp fine salt
- 1½ cups all-purpose flour, sifted, plus extra for dusting
- 2 tsp unsalted butter, melted
- Non-stick cooking spray

Filling
- 3 tbsp light brown sugar
- 1½ tsp ground cinnamon

Cream cheese glaze
- ¼ cup cream cheese at room temperature
- ¼ tsp vanilla extract
- Pinch of fine salt
- ¼ cup confectioner's sugar, sifted
- Low-fat milk, as needed

Directions:

For the dough:

1. In a small mixing bowl, dissolve the yeast in the warm water, and set aside for 5 minutes, or until foamy.

2. In a medium-sized mixing bowl, combine the granulated sugar, low-fat milk, large egg, fine salt, yeast mixture, and 1 cup of all-purpose flour. Whisk until smooth.

3. Stir in the remaining ½ cup all-purpose flour, and use a wooden spoon to mix, until it becomes difficult. Use your hands to gently knead, until it comes together, and shapes into a ball (the dough will be a little sticky).

4. Place the dough onto a lightly floured surface, and knead for 8 minutes, until it is completely smooth and elastic.

5. Lightly coat a large mixing bowl with ½ tsp of the melted butter. Place the dough in the bowl, turning once to grease all over. Cover with a damp kitchen towel. Let the dough rise for 1 hour in a warm place, until doubled in size.

6. Coat a 7-inch round cake pan with non-stick cooking spray, and set aside.

For the filling:

7. In a small mixing bowl, add together the brown sugar and cinnamon, and mix to combine.

8. Once it has risen, transfer the dough to a lightly floured surface, and use a rolling pin to roll into a rectangle, ¼ inch thick. Brush with the remaining 1½ tsp melted butter, and sprinkle with the cinnamon and sugar mixture.

9. Cut into 7 strips, 1-inch wide, and roll each strip tightly. Place the rolls into the prepared pan, spiral side up. Cover with a damp kitchen towel, and allow to rise for 20 to 40 minutes, until the rolls have doubled in size.

10. Preheat the air fryer to 270°F, or 130°C.

11. Place the pan in the air fryer basket. Bake for 20 to 22 minutes, until golden brown. Allow to cool in the pan for 5 minutes.

For the glaze:

12. In a small mixing bowl, combine the cream cheese, vanilla extract, and fine salt, and whisk until smooth.

13. Whisk in the sifted confectioner's sugar until fully incorporated.

14. Add the low-fat milk 1 tsp at a time, until the mixture is pourable, but still thick.

15. Spread the glaze over the slightly warm cinnamon rolls, making sure the tops of the rolls are completely covered.

16. Serve warm.

BREAKFASTS

RED PEPPER HASH

COOK TIME: 45 MIN | SERVES: 1

Ingredients:

- ½ zucchini, cut into pieces
- ¼ cup jarred roasted red peppers, rinsed, dried, and chopped
- 1 cup whole-grain bread, cut into pieces
- 1 tbsp tomato paste
- 2 tsp olive oil, plus extra for drizzling
- 1 tsp red wine vinegar
- 1 tsp crushed red pepper flakes
- 2 large eggs
- Olive oil cooking spray
- Pinch sea salt
- 1 tbsp rosemary, chopped

Directions:

1. Preheat the air fryer to 400°F, or 200°C.

2. In a 3-cup oven-proof bowl, add together the zucchini pieces, chopped peppers, bread pieces, tomato paste, olive oil, red wine vinegar, and crushed red pepper flakes. Mix to combine.

3. Place the bowl in the air-fryer basket, and cook for 8 to 10 minutes, stirring occasionally, until the zucchini is tender, and the edges of the bread begin to brown.

4. Remove the basket from the air fryer, and reduce the temperature to 250°F, or 120°C. Make two shallow indentations in the vegetable mixture with the back of a spoon.

5. Crack 1 egg into each indentation, then lightly spray with olive oil cooking spray, and sprinkle with sea salt.

6. Return the basket to the air fryer, and cook for 6 to 8 minutes, until the egg whites are opaque, but still slightly jiggly. Turn off the air fryer, and allow the eggs to sit for 6 to 8 minutes, until the whites are set. Sprinkle the eggs with chopped rosemary, and drizzle with the extra olive oil. Serve warm.

BREAKFASTS

BLUEBERRY BUNS

COOK TIME: 15 MIN | MAKES: 6

Ingredients:

- 1 cup all-purpose flour, plus more for dusting
- 2½ tbsp unsalted cold butter, cubed
- 1 tbsp granulated sugar
- 1½ tsp baking powder
- ¼ tsp fine salt
- ½ cup whole milk
- ½ cup blueberries
- ¼ cup dark chocolate chips
- Olive oil cooking spray

Directions:

1. Preheat the air fryer to 270°F, or 130°C.
2. Place a parchment liner in the air fryer basket.
3. In a large mixing bowl, combine the all-purpose flour, unsalted cold butter, granulated sugar, baking powder, and fine salt.
4. With clean hands, work the ingredients together until the mixture resembles breadcrumbs.
5. Make a well in the center of the mixture, and pour in the whole milk.
6. Combine the mixture with your hands until it forms a thick dough.
7. Transfer the dough onto a well-floured work surface.
8. Add the blueberries and dark chocolate chips, and gently work them through the dough, taking care to not squash the berries.
9. Form the dough into a ball, and flatten it out slightly with your fingertips, making sure not to crush the berries.
10. Cut into 6 wedges, and place them on the liner in the air fryer basket.
11. Spray lightly with olive oil cooking spray, and bake for 5 minutes.
12. Move the buns around, and bake for another 5 minutes.
13. Flip the buns over, and bake for a further 5 minutes. Serve warm.

Serve buns with: whipped cream, jam, shredded cheddar cheese, or butter.

SNACKS & APPETIZERS

SNACKS & APPETIZERS

LEMON GARBANZO BEANS

COOK TIME: 15 MIN | MAKES: 1½ CUPS

INGREDIENTS:

- 1 (15 oz) can garbanzo beans, drained
- 2 tbsp avocado oil, divided
- 1 large lemon, juiced and zested
- Pinch of salt

DIRECTIONS:

1. Preheat the air fryer to 400°F, or 200°C.

2. Line the air fryer basket with parchment paper.

3. In a large mixing bowl, combine the drained garbanzo beans, 1 tbsp of avocado oil, lemon juice, lemon zest, and a pinch of salt. Toss to coat.

4. Place the garbanzo beans without the lemon juice into the lined air fryer basket, and roast for 15 minutes, until golden and crispy.

5. Transfer the garbanzo beans back into the large bowl with the lemon juice, and toss with the remaining 1 tbsp avocado oil before serving.

Flavor tip: you can use different spices in this recipe, like smoked paprika, ground black pepper, onion powder, or garlic powder.

SNACKS & APPETIZERS

ASIAN CHICKEN SKEWERS

COOK TIME: 30 MIN | SERVES: 4-6

Ingredients:

- 2 tbsp Thai green curry paste
- 1 tbsp light brown sugar
- 2 tsp oyster sauce
- 1 tsp lime zest
- 1 tbsp lime juice
- 2 tsp sunflower oil
- 12 oz boneless, skinless chicken breasts, cut into 12 thick strips
- 12 (6-inch) wooden skewers, soaked in water
- 3 tbsp cashew butter
- 2 tbsp basil, finely chopped

Directions:

1. Preheat the air fryer to 400°F, or 200°C.

2. In a large mixing bowl, add together the green curry paste, brown sugar, oyster sauce, lime zest, and lime juice. Whisk to combine. Transfer 2 tbsp of the green curry paste mixture to a medium-sized mixing bowl, and set aside.

3. Whisk the sunflower oil into the large bowl with the green curry paste mixture. Add the chicken strips, and toss to coat.

4. Weave the chicken slices evenly onto each skewer, leaving the bottom of the skewer exposed.

5. Arrange half of the skewers in the air fryer basket, spaced evenly apart. Arrange the remaining skewers on top, perpendicular to the bottom layer.

6. Place the basket into the air fryer, and cook for 6 to 8 minutes, until the chicken is browned.

7. Add the cashew butter into the reserved green curry paste mixture, and whisk until smooth. Adjust the consistency with hot water if it is too thick.

8. Transfer the skewers onto a serving platter, and sprinkle with chopped basil. Serve with the cashew nut sauce.

Tip: soaking the wooden skewers in water for up to an hour, or better, overnight, will prevent the skewers from burning in all methods of cooking.

SNACKS & APPETIZERS

SHRIMP WONTON

COOK TIME: 8 MIN | SERVES: 5

Ingredients:

- 4 oz plain cream cheese at room temperature
- ½ cup peeled and deveined shrimp, roughly chopped
- 2 spring onions, chopped
- 1 tbsp garlic, crushed
- 2 tsp dark soy sauce
- 15 wonton wrappers
- White of 1 large egg, beaten
- 5 tbsp sweet chili sauce, for dipping

Directions:

1. Preheat the air fryer to 340°F, or 170°C.

2. In a medium-sized mixing bowl, add together the plain cream cheese, chopped shrimp, chopped spring onions, crushed garlic, and dark soy sauce. Whisk to combine.

3. Working with one wonton wrapper at a time, place them on a clean surface, the points facing top and bottom, like a diamond.

4. Spoon 1 tbsp of the shrimp mixture onto the center of the wrapper. Run a pastry brush dipped in water along the edges of the wrapper.

5. Take one corner of the wrapper, and fold it up to the opposite corner, to form a triangle. Gently press out any air between the wrapper and filling, and seal the edges. Set aside, and repeat with the remaining wrappers and filling.

6. Brush both sides of the wontons with beaten egg white.

7. Working in batches, arrange a single layer of the wontons in the air fryer basket. Cook for 8 minutes, flipping half way, until golden brown and crispy. Serve hot, with the sweet chili sauce for dipping.

SNACKS & APPETIZERS

DRIED TOFU

COOK TIME: 45 MIN | MAKES: 24

Ingredients:

- 2 tbsp dark soy sauce
- 1 tsp sesame oil
- 1 tbsp apple cider vinegar
- 1 tbsp ketchup
- 2 tsp molasses
- 225g extra firm tofu, patted dry, and sliced into 24 thin slices
- Non-stick cooking spray

Directions:

1. In a shallow dish, add together the dark soy sauce, sesame oil, apple cider vinegar, ketchup, and molasses. Mix to combine.

2. Add the sliced tofu, and marinate for 30 minutes, or overnight, in the fridge.

3. Set the air fryer temperature to 180°F, or 82°C. Coat the fryer basket with nonstick cooking spray.

4. Pat the tofu slices dry with paper towels. Place in the fryer basket, and cook for 45 minutes, until brown and slightly crispy.

5. Transfer the dried tofu onto a platter, and allow it to cool completely before serving.

Substitution tip: you can use tempeh in place of the tofu.

SNACKS & APPETIZERS

DILL PICKLE CHIPS

COOK TIME: 8 MIN | SERVES: 4

Ingredients:

- 24 dill pickle slices
- 1/3 cup plain breadcrumbs
- 2 tbsp cornmeal
- 1 tsp barbeque seasoning
- 1 tbsp dried parsley
- 1 large egg, beaten
- Olive oil cooking spray

Buttermilk dressing:
- 1/3 cup buttermilk
- 3 tbsp light mayonnaise
- 3 tbsp chives, chopped
- ¾ tsp Cajun seasoning
- ⅛ tsp garlic powder
- ⅛ tsp onion powder
- ⅛ tsp sea salt
- Ground black pepper

Directions:

1. Preheat the air fryer to 400°F, or 200°C.

2. Place the pickle slices on paper towels to absorb the excess liquid, then pat dry.

3. In a medium-sized mixing bowl, add together the breadcrumbs, cornmeal, barbeque seasoning, and dried parsley. Mix to combine. Place the beaten egg in a small mixing bowl.

4. Working with one pickle slice at a time, coat it in the beaten egg, then in the breadcrumb mixture. Gently press the breadcrumbs onto the pickle slice to stick. Set aside on a work surface, and repeat with the remaining pickles. Spray both sides of the pickles with olive oil cooking spray.

5. Working in batches, arrange a single layer of the pickle chips in the air fryer basket. Cook for 8 minutes, flipping half way, until golden and crisp.

For the dressing:
6. In a small mixing bowl, combine the buttermilk, mayonnaise, chopped chives, Cajun seasoning, garlic powder, onion powder, sea salt, and ground black pepper to taste. Mix well, and serve alongside the pickles for dipping.

SNACKS & APPETIZERS

STUFFED PEPPERS

COOK TIME: 6-8 MIN | MAKES: 10

INGREDIENTS:

- 8 oz plain cream cheese at room temperature
- 1 cup panko breadcrumbs, divided
- 2 tbsp Italian seasoning
- 1 tsp crushed red pepper flakes
- 10 jalapeño peppers, halved and seeded

DIRECTIONS:

1. Preheat the air fryer to 370°F, or 187°C.

2. In a small mixing bowl, add together the cream cheese, ½ cup of panko breadcrumbs, dried Italian seasoning, and crushed red pepper flakes. Mix to combine.

3. Stuff the cream cheese mixture into the jalapeño halves.

4. Sprinkle the tops of the stuffed jalapeños with the remaining ½ cup of panko breadcrumbs.

5. Place the stuffed peppers in the air fryer basket, and fry for 6 to 8 minutes, until the peppers are softened, and the cream cheese is melted. Serve warm.

SNACKS & APPETIZERS

PEPPER POPCORN

COOK TIME: 10 MIN | SERVES: 2

Ingredients:

- Aluminum foil
- 2 tbsp sunflower oil
- ¼ cup popcorn kernels
- 1 tsp sea salt
- ½ tsp ground black pepper

Directions:

1. Preheat the air fryer to 380°F, or 190°C.

2. Cover the bottom of the air fryer basket with aluminum foil, and place it into the air fryer.

3. Drizzle sunflower oil over the top of the foil, and add the popcorn kernels.

4. Roast for 8 to 10 minutes, or until the popcorn stops popping.

5. Transfer the popcorn into a large bowl, and sprinkle with sea salt and ground black pepper before serving.

SNACKS & APPETIZERS

MEDITERRANEAN MEATBALLS

COOK TIME: 35 MIN | SERVES: 2

Ingredients:

- ¼ cup couscous
- 3 tbsp boiling water, plus 1 tbsp cold water
- ¾ cup plain Greek yogurt
- 2 tbsp dried mint
- ½ tbsp garlic, minced
- ½ tsp lime zest, plus 2 tsp lime juice
- ½ tsp sea salt, divided
- ¼ tsp ground black pepper, divided
- ½ tsp ground cumin
- ¼ tsp ground coriander
- 8 oz lean ground beef
- 1 tbsp almond butter

Directions:

1. Preheat the air fryer to 400°F, or 200°C.

2. In a large mixing bowl, add the couscous and boiling water together. Cover, and allow to sit for 15 minutes, until the couscous is tender, and all water has been absorbed.

3. In a small mixing bowl, add together the Greek yogurt, dried mint, minced garlic, lime zest and lime juice, ¼ tsp sea salt, and ⅛ tsp ground black pepper. Whisk to combine.

4. Into the large bowl with the couscous, add ¼ cup of the yogurt mixture, the ground cumin, ground coriander, remaining ¼ tsp sea salt, and remaining ⅛ tsp ground black pepper, Set the remaining yogurt mixture aside.

5. Break the ground beef into small pieces over the couscous mixture, and lightly knead with your hands until well combined. Roll the mixture into 12 meatballs.

6. Arrange the meatballs in the air-fryer basket, spaced evenly apart. Place the basket into the air fryer, and cook for 7 to 9 minutes, turning half way through cooking, until the meatballs are lightly browned.

7. Add the almond butter and 1 tbsp cold water into the reserved yogurt mixture. Whisk until smooth, and the sauce is slightly thick. Serve the meatballs with the yogurt sauce.

SNACKS & APPETIZERS

SWEET POTATO CHIPS

COOK TIME: 30 MIN | SERVES: 6

INGREDIENTS:

- 4 medium sweet potatoes, rinsed and thinly sliced
- 1 tsp fine salt
- 1 tsp ground black pepper
- 2 tbsp olive oil
- Hummus, for serving

DIRECTIONS:

1. Preheat the air fryer to 380°F, or 190°C.

2. In a large mixing bowl, combine the sliced sweet potatoes, fine salt, ground black pepper, and olive oil. Toss to coat.

3. Place the sweet potato slices into the air fryer, and spread them out in a single layer.

4. Fry for 10 minutes, stir, and then fry for another 10 minutes. Mix again, and fry for a final 5 to 10 minutes, or until the chips reach the desired crispiness. Repeat with any remaining sweet potato slices.

5. Serve with hummus for dipping.

Substitution tip: you can replace sweet potatoes with beets or carrots.

Flavor tip: add garlic and paprika to your hummus for extra flavor.

SNACKS & APPETIZERS

BROCCOLI DIP

COOK TIME: 20 MIN | SERVES: 3

Ingredients:

- ½ (12 oz) bag frozen kale, thawed
- ½ (12 oz) bag frozen broccoli florets, thawed, and finely chopped
- 2 spring onions, white and green parts finely chopped
- ½ cup unsalted peanuts
- ½ cup unsweetened almond milk
- 3 tbsp lemon juice
- 1½ tbsp low-sodium soy sauce
- 2 tsp all-purpose flour
- 1 tsp No-Salt Spice Blend

Directions:

1. Preheat the air fryer to 360°F, or 182°C.

2. Place the kale, chopped broccoli florets, and chopped spring onions in a baking pan that can fit into your air fryer. Set aside.

3. In a blender, combine the unsalted peanuts, almond milk, lemon juice, low-sodium soy sauce, all-purpose flour, and no-salt spice blend, and blend on high until smooth. Pour the blended mixture over the kale, broccoli, and spring onions.

4. Place the baking pan in the air fryer, and bake for 20 minutes, mixing every 5 minutes during cooking. Serve warm.

Substitution tip: If you're allergic to nuts, swap the peanuts for sunflower seeds, and the almond milk for coconut milk.

SNACKS & APPETIZERS

GARLIC POTATO WEDGES

COOK TIME: 20-25 MIN | MAKES: 16

Ingredients:

- 2 russet potatoes, washed
- 1 tbsp olive oil
- 1 tbsp garlic powder
- ¼ cup Romano cheese, grated
- ¼ tsp fine salt
- ¼ tsp ground black pepper

Directions:

1. Preheat the air fryer to 400°F, or 200°C.

2. Cut the potatoes into thin wedges, and place them in a large mixing bowl.

3. Drizzle the olive oil over the potato wedges, and toss to coat.

4. Sprinkle the garlic powder, grated Romano cheese, fine salt, and ground black pepper over the potatoes, and toss again.

5. Place the seasoned potato wedges in the air fryer basket, and fry for 20 to 25 minutes, stirring half way through, until golden and crispy.

6. Serve warm.

SNACKS & APPETIZERS

ITALIAN RICE BALLS

COOK TIME: 9 MIN | SERVES: 4

Ingredients:

- 2 (2.75 oz) mild Italian sausage, casings removed
- 4½ cups frozen riced broccoli
- ½ tsp sea salt
- 1¼ cups marinara sauce
- 1 cup mozzarella cheese, shredded
- Non-stick cooking spray
- 2 large eggs
- ½ cup plain breadcrumbs
- 2 tbsp Parmesan cheese, grated
- Olive oil spray

Directions:

1. Heat a large, heavy bottom pan over medium-high heat. Add the sausage meat, and cook for 4 to 5 minutes, breaking the meat up with a fork, until cooked through.

2. Add the riced broccoli, sea salt, and ¼ cup of the marinara sauce. Mix to combine. Reduce the heat to medium, and cook for 6 to 7 minutes, stirring occasionally, until the riced broccoli is tender, and heated through.

3. Remove from the heat, and add the shredded mozzarella cheese. Mix, and allow to cool for 3 to 4 minutes, or until it's easy to handle with your hands.

4. Coat a ¼-cup measuring cup with non-stick cooking spray, and pack tightly with the broccoli mixture, leveling the top.

5. Use a small spoon to scoop it out onto the palm of your hand, and roll it into a ball. Set aside on a dish. Repeat with the remaining broccoli mixture to make 12 balls.

6. In a small mixing bowl, beat the large eggs with 1 tbsp of water, until smooth. In a second bowl, combine the plain breadcrumbs and grated Parmesan cheese.

7. Working with one at a time, dip a broccoli ball in the beaten egg, then in the breadcrumbs. Transfer to a work surface and lightly spray with olive oil. Repeat with the remaining broccoli balls.

8. Preheat the air fryer to 400°F, or 200°C.

9. Working in batches, arrange a single layer of the broccoli balls in the air fryer basket. Cook for 9 minutes, flipping half way, until the breadcrumbs are golden, and the center is hot.

10. Meanwhile, heat the remaining 1 cup of marinara for serving.

11. Serve the rice balls with the warm marinara for dipping.

CHEESY BACON STICKS

COOK TIME: 8 MIN | MAKES: 6

Ingredients:

- 1 tbsp water
- 6 egg roll wrappers
- 6 tsp tomato sauce
- 18 bacon slices
- 3 mozzarella sticks, halved
- Olive oil spray

Directions:

1. Preheat the air fryer to 400°F, or 200°C. Line the bottom of the air fryer basket with a parchment liner.

2. Place the water in a small bowl, and set it aside.

3. Lay one egg roll wrapper on the counter in a diamond shape, with the point facing you.

4. Place 1 tsp of tomato sauce in the center, followed by 3 bacon slices, and then half a mozzarella stick.

5. Fold the two sides inwards, and then take the point that is pointing towards you, and fold it inwards to make the wrapper look like an envelope.

6. Using a pastry brush, moisten the open edges of the wrapper with water.

7. Roll from the bottom, folded end of the wrapper towards the open point, until you reach the top. The moistened part should now be sealed to the rest of the wrapper. Repeat with the remaining wrappers.

8. Place the wrapped sticks in the air fryer, in a single layer on the parchment liner.

9. Spray lightly with olive oil spray, and fry for 4 minutes. Turn the sticks over, and spray again. Fry for another 3 to 4 minutes, until golden and crispy. Serve warm.

SNACKS & APPETIZERS

MINI BEEF BURGERS

COOK TIME: 9 MIN | SERVES: 2

Ingredients:

- 10 oz ground beef
- ½ tsp onion powder
- ¼ tsp fine salt
- ¼ tsp ground black pepper
- 2 tbsp pitted dates, finely chopped
- 2 tbsp water
- 1 tsp garlic, crushed
- 2 tsp light brown sugar
- 1½ tsp thyme, chopped
- 1 tsp parsley, chopped
- 1 tsp lime juice
- ¼ cup feta cheese, crumbled
- 4 soft, white dinner rolls
- 4 iceberg lettuce leaves

Directions:

1. Preheat the air fryer to 400°F, or 200°C.

2. Divide the ground beef into 4 balls, and gently flatten each ball into a patty. Press the center of each patty with your fingertips to create a depression. Sprinkle with onion powder, and season with fine salt and ground black pepper.

3. Arrange the patties in the air fryer basket, spaced evenly apart. Place the basket in the air fryer, and cook for 9 minutes, flipping and rotating the patties half way through cooking, until lightly browned.

4. In a microwave-safe bowl, combine the chopped dates, water, crushed garlic, brown sugar, chopped thyme, chopped parsley, lime juice, and a pinch of fine salt. Microwave for 1 minute, until the dates soften. Use a fork to mash the dates against the side of the bowl to thicken the chutney.

5. Transfer the patties onto a plate, and top with crumbled feta cheese. Spread 2 tsp of the homemade chutney on the bottom of each roll, and top with 1 iceberg lettuce leaf and a patty. Place the roll tops, and serve.

FISH & SEAFOOD

FISH & SEAFOOD

SPICY SALMON

COOK TIME: 8 MIN | SERVES: 4

Ingredients:

For the salmon:
- 1 tbsp smoked paprika
- ½ tsp crushed red pepper flakes
- 1 tsp garlic powder
- 1 tsp dried parsley
- 1 teaspoon dried thyme
- ¾ tsp fine salt
- ⅛ tsp ground black pepper
- Olive oil spray
- 4 (6 oz) salmon fillets

For the cucumber salsa:
- ¼ red onion, chopped
- 1½ tbsp lime juice
- 1 lime, zested
- 1 tsp olive oil
- ¼ tsp plus ⅛ tsp fine salt
- Ground black pepper
- 1 medium cucumber, diced
- 1 ripe avocado, pitted and diced

Directions:

For the salmon:

1. Preheat the air fryer to 400°F, or 200°C.

2. In a small mixing bowl, add together the smoked paprika, crushed red pepper flakes, garlic powder, dried parsley, dried thyme, fine salt, and ground black pepper. Mix to combine. Spray both sides of the salmon fillets with olive oil spray, and rub the oil all over. Coat the salmon generously with the spice mix.

3. Working in batches, place the salmon fillets skin side down in the air fryer basket. Cook for 5 to 8 minutes, or until the fish flakes easily with a fork. While the salmon is cooking, prepare the cucumber salsa.

For the cucumber salsa:

4. In a medium-sized mixing bowl, add together the chopped red onion, lime juice, lime zest, olive oil, fine salt, and ground black pepper. Mix to combine. Allow it to stand for 5 minutes, then add the diced cucumber and avocado.

5. Serve the salmon fillets topped with the cucumber salsa.

FISH & SEAFOOD

MINT & LIME HADDOCK

COOK TIME: 16 MIN | SERVES: 2

Ingredients:

- Aluminum foil
- 1/3 cup panko breadcrumbs
- 1 tsp sunflower oil
- 1 small onion, finely chopped
- ½ tbsp garlic, minced
- 1 tbsp mint, chopped
- Fine Salt
- Ground black pepper
- 1 tbsp cilantro, finely chopped
- 1 tbsp lite mayonnaise
- Yolk of 1 large egg
- ¼ tsp lime zest, plus lime wedges for serving
- 2 (10 oz) skinless haddock fillets

Directions:

1. Preheat the air fryer to 300°F, or 148°C. Line the air fryer basket all over with aluminum foil. Lightly coat the foil with sunflower oil.

2. In a microwave-safe mixing bowl, toss the panko breadcrumbs with sunflower oil, until well coated. Add the chopped onion, minced garlic, chopped mint, and fine salt and ground black pepper to taste. Mix to combine.

3. Microwave the breadcrumb mixture for 2 minutes, stirring frequently, until the panko is a light golden brown. Transfer the mixture to a shallow dish, and allow it to cool slightly. Add in the chopped cilantro, and mix.

4. In a small mixing bowl, add together the lite mayonnaise, egg yolk, lime zest, and some ground black pepper. Mix to combine.

5. Pat the haddock dry with paper towels, and season with fine salt and ground black pepper to taste.

6. Place the haddock fillets on a plate, and brush evenly with the mayonnaise mixture on one side. Working with 1 fillet at a time, coat the side of the haddock with the mayonnaise mixture in the panko mixture, pressing gently to make sure the breadcrumbs stick.

7. Place the haddock fillets crumb side up in the prepared air fryer basket, spaced evenly apart. Place the basket in the air fryer, and cook for 12 to 16 minutes, or until the fish flakes easily with a fork. Serve with lime wedges.

FISH & SEAFOOD

ORANGE HALIBUT

COOK TIME: 20 MIN | SERVES: 2

Ingredients:

- 1 small eggplant, cut into pieces
- 6 oz grape tomatoes
- 3 spring onions, cut lengthwise
- 2 tbsp olive oil
- Fine salt
- Ground black pepper
- 12 oz skinless halibut fillets, cut into cubes
- 2 tsp honey
- 2 tsp ground coriander
- 1 tsp orange zest, plus 1 tsp orange juice
- 4 (6-inch) wooden skewers, soaked in water
- ½ tbsp garlic, minced
- ½ tsp ground cumin
- 1 tbsp cilantro, chopped

Directions:

1. Preheat the air fryer to 400°F, or 200°C.

2. In a large mixing bowl, combine the eggplant pieces, grape tomatoes, cut spring onion, 1 tbsp olive oil, and fine salt and ground black pepper to taste. Transfer to the air fryer basket. Place the basket in the air fryer, and cook for 14 minutes, until the vegetables have softened and browned. Transfer the vegetables to a cutting board, and set aside to cool slightly.

3. Pat the halibut cubes dry with paper towels. In a medium-sized mixing bowl, add together 1 tsp olive oil, 1 tsp honey, 1 tsp coriander, ½ tsp orange zest, some fine salt and ground black pepper, and the halibut cubes. Mix to combine. Thread the halibut cubes onto the skewers, leaving space between each piece.

4. Place the skewers in the now empty air fryer basket, spaced evenly apart. Return the basket to the air fryer, and cook for 6 to 8 minutes, flipping and rotating the skewers half way through cooking, until the halibut has browned.

5. In a small, microwave-safe mixing bowl, add together the remaining 2 tsp olive oil, remaining 1 tsp honey, remaining 1 tsp coriander, remaining ½ tsp orange zest, orange juice, minced garlic, ground cumin, and fine salt and ground black pepper to taste. Mix to combine.

6. Microwave for 30 seconds, stirring once, until fragrant.

7. Roughly chop the cooked vegetables, and place them into the bowl with the dressing, along with any accumulated juices. Gently toss to combine. Mix in the chopped cilantro, and season with fine salt and ground black pepper to taste. Serve the skewers with the vegetables.

FISH & SEAFOOD

LIME TROUT

COOK TIME: 15 MIN | SERVES: 4

Ingredients:

- 4 trout fillets
- 2 tbsp sunflower oil
- ½ tsp fine salt
- 1 tsp ground black pepper
- 1 tbsp garlic, crushed
- 1 lime, sliced, plus additional wedges for serving

Directions:

1. Preheat the air fryer to 380°F, or 193°C.

2. Coat each trout fillet with sunflower oil on both sides, and season with fine salt and ground black pepper. Place the trout fillets in an even layer in the air fryer basket.

3. Spread the crushed garlic over the top of each trout fillet, then top the garlic with lime slices. Cook for 12 to 15 minutes, or until the fish flakes easily with a fork.

4. Serve with lime wedges.

Substitution tip: you can use oranges, lemons, or grapefruit for this recipe.

FISH & SEAFOOD

COD & GARBANZO SALAD

COOK TIME: 16 MIN | SERVES: 2

Ingredients:

- Aluminum foil
- ¾ tsp ground coriander
- ½ tsp ground cumin
- ¼ tsp ground ginger
- ⅛ tsp ground nutmeg
- Sea salt
- Ground black pepper
- 2 (8-10 oz) skinless cod fillets
- 4 tsp olive oil, plus extra for drizzling
- 1 (15 oz) can garbanzo beans, rinsed
- 1 tbsp grapefruit juice, plus grapefruit wedges for serving
- 1 tsp chili paste
- ½ tsp honey
- 2 parsnips, peeled and shredded
- 2 tbsp parsley, chopped

Directions:

1. Preheat the air fryer to 300°F, or 148°C. Line the air fryer basket all over with aluminum foil. Lightly coat the foil with olive oil.

2. In a small mixing bowl, add together the ground coriander, ground cumin, ground ginger, ground nutmeg, and sea salt and ground black pepper to taste. Mix to combine.

3. Pat the cod fillets dry with paper towels. Rub each fillet with 1 tsp olive oil, and sprinkle all over with the spice mixture. Place the seasoned fillets in the prepared basket, spaced evenly apart. Place the basket in the air fryer, and cook for 12 to 16 minutes, or until the cod fillets flake easily with a fork.

4. Place the garbanzo beans in a microwave-safe bowl, and heat them in the microwave for 2 minutes. Stir in the remaining 1 tbsp olive oil, the grapefruit juice, chili paste, and honey, and sea salt and ground black pepper to taste. Add the shredded parsnips and 1 tbsp chopped parsley, and mix to combine.

5. Carefully remove the cod fillets from the air fryer, and transfer them onto individual plates. Sprinkle with the remaining 1 tbsp chopped parsley, and drizzle with extra olive oil. Serve with the garbanzo bean salad and grapefruit wedges.

FISH & SEAFOOD

PEAR SCALLOPS

COOK TIME: 10 MIN | SERVES: 2

INGREDIENTS:

- 12 oz sea scallops, tendons removed
- 5 tsp sunflower oil
- 2 tsp ginger, grated
- 1 tsp honey
- ½ tsp ground turmeric
- ½ tsp dried basil
- ¼ tsp fine salt
- 1 tsp lemon zest, plus 1 tbsp lemon juice, plus lemon wedges for serving
- 1 small onion, thinly sliced
- 1 Thai chili, stemmed and thinly sliced
- 1 cucumber, cut into ribbons
- 2 pears, peeled, pitted, and thinly sliced
- ¼ cup parsley, chopped
- 2 tbsp pumpkin seeds, roasted

DIRECTIONS:

1. Preheat the air fryer to 400°F, or 200°C.

2. Dry the scallops between two clean dish towels. Allow the scallops to sit for 10 minutes at room temperature.

3. In a small mixing bowl, add together the sunflower oil, grated ginger, honey, ground turmeric, dried basil, and fine salt. Whisk to combine. Microwave for 30 seconds, until fragrant, and allow to cool slightly.

4. In a large mixing bowl, add together 1 tbsp of the oil mixture, lemon zest, and lemon juice, and whisk to combine. Add the sliced onion and Thai chili, mix, and set aside.

5. Coat the scallops with the remaining oil mixture in a separate bowl. Place the scallops in the air fryer basket, spaced evenly apart. Place the basket into the air fryer, and cook for 6 to 10 minutes, flipping the scallops half way through cooking, until they are firm to the touch, and spotty brown.

6. Add the cucumber ribbons, sliced pears, chopped parsley, and roasted pumpkin seeds into the bowl with the remaining dressing, and toss gently to combine. Season with fine salt and ground black pepper to taste.

7. Divide the pear salad between individual serving plates, and top with the scallops. Serve with lemon wedges.

FISH & SEAFOOD

SRIRACHA SHRIMP TORTILLAS

COOK TIME: 10 MIN | SERVES: 2

Ingredients:

- Aluminum foil
- ½ cup apple cider vinegar
- 2 tbsp light brown sugar, divided
- ½ tsp fine salt, divided
- ½ small red onion, thinly sliced
- Olive oil cooking spray
- 12 oz large shrimp, peeled, deveined, and tails removed
- 2 tbsp sriracha chili sauce
- 1 tbsp olive oil
- ½ tsp smoked paprika
- ¼ cup plain Greek yogurt
- 1 tbsp lemon juice, plus lemon wedges for serving
- 1½ cups bok choy, shredded
- ¼ cup parsley, chopped, plus extra leaves for serving
- 6 (6-inch) corn tortillas, warmed

Directions:

1. Preheat the air fryer to 400°F, or 200°C. Cover the air fryer basket in aluminum foil.

2. In a medium-sized, microwave-safe mixing bowl, combine the apple cider vinegar, 1½ tbsp brown sugar, and ¼ tsp fine salt, and microwave for 2 to 3 minutes, until steaming. Whisk until the sugar and salt have dissolved.

3. Add the sliced onion to the hot brine mixture, and press to submerge the onions completely. Allow to sit for 45 minutes. Reserve 2 tbsp of the brine, and drain the onions.

4. Spray the air fryer basket with olive oil cooking spray. Halve the shrimp lengthwise. In a large mixing bowl, add together the sriracha chili sauce, olive oil, smoked paprika, remaining 1½ tsp brown sugar, and remaining ¼ tsp fine salt. Whisk to combine. Add the shrimp, and toss to coat.

5. Place the shrimp in an even layer in the prepared basket. Place the basket into the air fryer, and cook for 6 to 10 minutes, tossing half way through cooking, until the shrimp are opaque throughout.

6. In a small mixing bowl, add together the Greek yogurt and lemon juice, and whisk to combine. In a separate bowl, toss the shredded bok choy with the chopped parsley, and the reserved 2 tbsp brine. Serve the shrimp on warmed tortillas, with bok choy, pickled onions, the Greek yogurt mixture, lemon wedges, and extra chopped parsley.

FISH & SEAFOOD

POTATO COD CAKES

COOK TIME: 10 MIN | SERVES: 4

Ingredients:

For the cod cakes:
- 3 large eggs
- 12 oz raw cod fillet, flaked apart with two forks
- ¼ cup whole milk
- ½ cup instant mashed potatoes
- 2 tsp sunflower oil
- 1/3 cup dill, chopped
- 1 small onion, finely chopped
- ½ tbsp garlic, minced
- ¾ cup plus 2 tbsp plain breadcrumbs
- 1 tsp lime juice
- 1 tsp fine salt
- ½ tsp dried oregano
- ¼ tsp ground black pepper
- Olive oil spray

Lime and dill garlic sauce:
- 5 tbsp lite mayonnaise
- 1 tsp garlic, crushed
- ½ lime, juiced
- 1 tbsp dill, chopped

Directions:

For the cod cakes:

1. Preheat the air fryer to 350°F, or 176°C.

2. In a medium-sized mixing bowl, beat 2 large eggs. Add in the flaked cod, whole milk, instant mashed potatoes, sunflower oil, chopped dill, chopped onion, minced garlic, 2 tbsp plain breadcrumbs, lime juice, fine salt, dried oregano, and ground black pepper. Mix to combine, and place in the fridge for 30 minutes.

3. Measure out about 3½ tbsp of the fish mixture, and roll it in your hands to form a ball. Repeat with the remaining mixture to make 12 balls.

4. In a small mixing bowl, beat the last egg. In a separate bowl, place the remaining ¾ cup of plain breadcrumbs. Dip the fish cakes in the beaten egg, and then coat in the breadcrumbs. Place them on a clean surface, and spray both sides with olive oil cooking spray.

5. Working in batches, place a single layer of the fish cakes in the air fryer basket. Cook for 10 minutes, flipping half way through, until golden. In the meantime, prepare the lime and dill garlic sauce.

Lime and dill garlic sauce:

6. In a small mixing bowl, add together the lite mayonnaise, crushed garlic, lime juice, and chopped dill. Mix to combine.

7. Serve the fish cakes with the lemon and dill garlic sauce for dipping.

FISH & SEAFOOD

CRUMBED CRAB

COOK TIME: 10 MIN | MAKES: 4

Ingredients:

For the cold sauce:
- ¾ cup lite mayonnaise
- 2 tsp Dijon mustard
- 1½ tsp whole-grain mustard
- 1 tsp apple cider vinegar
- ¼ tsp chili sauce
- 1 tsp capers, drained and chopped
- ¼ tsp fine salt
- ⅛ tsp ground black pepper

For the crumbed crab:
- 1 cup plain breadcrumbs, divided
- 2 tbsp lite mayonnaise
- 1 spring onion, finely chopped
- 6 oz crab meat
- 2 tbsp liquid eggs in a carton
- 2 tsp lime juice
- ½ tsp red pepper flakes
- ½ tsp Cajun seasoning
- Olive oil spray

Directions:

To make the cold sauce:

1. In a small mixing bowl, add together the lite mayonnaise, Dijon mustard, whole-grain mustard, apple cider vinegar, chili sauce, chopped capers, fine salt, and ground black pepper. Whisk to combine.

2. Place in the fridge for 1 hour before serving.

To make the crab cakes:

3. Heat the air fryer to 400°F, or 200°C. Line the air fryer basket with parchment liner.

4. In a large mixing bowl, add together ½ cup breadcrumbs, the lite mayonnaise, and the chopped spring onions. Mix to combine. Place the other ½ cup breadcrumbs aside in a small bowl.

5. In a large mixing bowl, add together the crab meat, liquid eggs, lime juice, red pepper flakes, and Cajun seasoning. Mix to combine.

6. Divide the crab meat mixture into 4 equal portions, and form it into patties.

7. Coat each patty with the remaining breadcrumbs. Place the coated patties on the liner in the air fryer basket in a single layer.

8. Lightly spray with olive oil cooking spray, and fry for 5 minutes. Flip the crab over, and fry for another 5 minutes, until golden. Serve with the cold sauce.

FISH & SEAFOOD

HADDOCK SANDWICH

COOK TIME: 17 MIN | SERVES: 2

INGREDIENTS:

For the tartar sauce
- ½ cup lite mayonnaise
- 2 tbsp red onion, minced
- 1 dill pickle, finely chopped
- 2 tsp pickle juice
- ¼ tsp fine salt
- ⅛ tsp ground black pepper

For the haddock:
- 2 tbsp all-purpose flour
- 1 large egg, lightly beaten
- 1 cup panko breadcrumbs
- 2 tsp Cajun seasoning
- 2 haddock fillets
- Olive oil spray
- 2 dinner rolls

DIRECTIONS:

To make the tartar sauce:
1. In a small mixing bowl, add together the lite mayonnaise, minced red onion, chopped pickle, pickle juice, fine salt, and ground black pepper. Mix to combine. Place the tartar sauce in the fridge until serving.

To make the fish:
2. Preheat the air fryer to 400°F, or 200°C. Line the air fryer basket with parchment liner.

3. Place the all-purpose flour on a plate, and set it aside.

4. Put the lightly beaten egg in a medium-sized, shallow bowl.

5. In another shallow bowl, add together the panko breadcrumbs and Cajun seasoning, and mix to combine.

6. Coat the haddock fillets in the all-purpose flour, then dip them in the beaten egg. Then press the haddock fillets into the panko breadcrumb mixture.

7. Place the prepared haddock fillets in the lined air fryer basket in a single layer.

8. Spray lightly with olive oil cooking spray, and fry for 8 minutes. Carefully flip the fillets, spray with more olive oil cooking spray, and fry for another 9 minutes, until golden and crispy.

9. Place each cooked haddock fillet in a dinner roll, top with some tartar sauce, and serve.

FISH & SEAFOOD

SHRIMP FETA POCKETS

COOK TIME: 8 MIN | SERVES: 4

Ingredients:

- 1 lb. large shrimp, peeled and deveined
- 2 tbsp olive oil
- 1 tsp dried parsley
- ½ tsp dried thyme
- ½ tsp garlic powder
- ¼ tsp onion powder
- ½ tsp fine salt
- ¼ tsp ground black pepper
- 4 whole-wheat pitas
- 4 oz herbed feta cheese, crumbled
- 1 cup Romaine lettuce, shredded
- 1 Roma tomato, diced
- ¼ cup pitted black olives, sliced
- 1 lime

Directions:

1. Preheat the air fryer to 380°F, or 190°C.

2. In a medium-sized mixing bowl, add together the cleaned shrimp, olive oil, dried parsley, dried thyme, garlic powder, onion powder, fine salt, and ground black pepper. Mix to combine.

3. Place the seasoned shrimp in a single layer in the air fryer basket, and cook for 6 to 8 minutes, or until cooked through.

4. Remove from the air fryer, and divide into the warmed pitas, with crumbled herbed feta cheese, shredded Romaine lettuce, diced tomato, sliced olives, and a squeeze of lime.

Flavor tip: add 1 tbsp of dark soy sauce in step two.

FISH & SEAFOOD

SMOKED PAPRIKA FLOUNDER

COOK TIME: 15 MIN | SERVES: 4

Ingredients:

- 1 large carrot, peeled, and diced small
- 1 large parsnip, peeled, and diced small
- 1 turnip, diced small
- ¼ cup sunflower oil
- 2 tsp fine salt, divided
- 4 flounder fillets
- ½ tsp onion powder
- 1 tbsp garlic, minced
- 1 lime, sliced, plus additional wedges for serving.

Directions:

1. Preheat the air fryer to 380°F, or 190°C.

2. In a small mixing bowl, combine the diced carrot, diced parsnip, diced turnip, sunflower oil, and 1 tsp fine salt. Toss to coat.

3. Season the flounder fillets with the remaining 1 tsp fine salt, and the onion powder, then place them into the air fryer basket in a single layer.

4. Spread the minced garlic on top of each flounder fillet, then cover with lime slices.

5. Place the prepared vegetables into the air fryer basket, around and on top of the flounder fillets. Roast for 15 minutes.

6. Serve with additional lime wedges.

FISH & SEAFOOD

HARISSA TILAPIA

COOK TIME: 14 MIN | SERVES: 2

INGREDIENTS:

- 12 oz Brussels sprouts, trimmed and halved
- 1 large leek, halved lengthwise, and sliced
- 3 tbsp sunflower oil, divided
- ½ tsp sea salt, divided
- 4 tsp harissa paste
- 2 (4 to 6 oz) skinless tilapia fillets
- 1 tsp grated lime zest, plus lime wedges for serving

DIRECTIONS:

1. Preheat the air fryer to 400°F, or 200°C.

2. In a large mixing bowl, combine the halved Brussels sprouts, sliced leek, 2 tbsp sunflower oil, and ¼ tsp sea salt. Toss to coat. Arrange the seasoned vegetables in an even layer in the air-fryer basket. Place the basket into the air fryer, and cook for 10 minutes, stirring the vegetables half way through cooking.

3. In a small mixing bowl, add together the harissa paste, remaining 1 tbsp sunflower oil, and remaining ¼ tsp sea salt, and mix to combine.

4. Pat the tilapia fillets dry with paper towels, and rub with the harissa paste mixture. Stir the vegetables, and place the tilapia fillets on top, spaced evenly apart. Return the basket to the air fryer, and cook for 8 to 14 minutes, until the tilapia fillets are lightly browned, and flake easily with a fork.

5. Transfer the tilapia fillets to a serving platter. Mix the lime zest into the vegetables, and season with sea salt and ground black pepper to taste. Transfer the vegetables to the platter with the tilapia fillets, and serve with lime wedges.

CAJUN-SPICED CATFISH

COOK TIME: 20 MIN | SERVES: 2

Ingredients:

- ½ cup fine cornmeal
- 2 tbsp all-purpose flour
- ¾ tsp fine salt
- 1 tsp smoked paprika
- 1 tsp Cajun seasoning
- ¼ tsp garlic powder
- ¼ tsp onion powder
- ¼ tsp ground black pepper
- 2 catfish fillets, cut in half
- Olive oil cooking spray

Directions:

1. Preheat the air fryer to 400°F, or 200°C. Line the air fryer basket with parchment liner.

2. In a zip-top bag, combine the fine cornmeal, all-purpose flour, fine salt, smoked paprika, Cajun seasoning, garlic powder, onion powder, and ground black pepper. Close the bag, and shake to mix.

3. Rinse the catfish fillets, and pat dry with paper towels.

4. Place the catfish fillets in the zip-top bag with the seasoning, seal, and give it a gentle shake to coat.

5. Place the coated catfish on the liner in the fryer basket, and fry for 10 minutes.

6. Open the basket, and spray the catfish filets with olive oil cooking spray. Flip the fish, and spray the other side with olive oil cooking spray. Continue to fry for another 7 to 10 minutes, until golden and crispy. Serve warm.

FISH & SEAFOOD

CHINESE SPICE TUNA

COOK TIME: 9 MIN | SERVES: 4

Ingredients:

- 1 tsp garlic powder
- ½ tsp fine salt
- ½ tsp Chinese five-spice powder
- ¼ tsp dried oregano
- 4 tuna steaks
- 2 tbsp sunflower oil
- 1 lime, quartered

Directions:

1. Preheat the air fryer to 380°F, or 193°C.

2. In a small mixing bowl, add together the garlic powder, fine salt, Chinese five-spice powder, and oregano, and mix to combine.

3. Coat the tuna steaks with sunflower oil, and season both sides with the seasoning blend. Place the tuna steaks in a single layer in the air fryer basket.

4. Cook for 5 minutes, then flip, and cook for an additional 3 to 4 minutes. Serve with your choice of side.

POULTRY

POULTRY

BBQ CHICKEN & SLAW

COOK TIME: 20 MIN | SERVES: 2

Ingredients:

- 3 cups shredded coleslaw mix
- Fine salt
- Ground black pepper
- 2 (12 oz) bone-in chicken breasts
- 1 tsp olive oil
- 2 tbsp sweet barbecue sauce, plus extra for serving
- 2 tbsp lite mayonnaise
- 2 tbsp sour cream
- 1 tsp apple cider vinegar, plus extra for seasoning
- ¼ tsp granulated sugar
- Aluminum foil

Directions:

1. Preheat the air fryer to 350°F, or 176°C.

2. Place the coleslaw mix and ¼ tsp fine salt in a colander, toss, and set over a bowl. Allow it to sit for 30 minutes, until wilted. Rinse, drain, and pat dry with a dish towel.

3. Dry the chicken breasts with paper towels, and rub each breast with olive oil. Season with fine salt and ground black pepper to taste.

4. Arrange the breasts skin side down in the air fryer basket, spaced evenly apart. Place the basket in the air fryer, and cook for 10 minutes. Flip and rotate the breasts. Using a pastry brush, coat the skin side with the sweet barbecue sauce. Return the basket to the air fryer, and cook for 10 to 15 minutes, until the chicken breasts are well browned and fully cooked.

5. Transfer the cooked chicken to a serving platter, cover with aluminum foil, and allow to rest for 5 minutes.

6. While the chicken rests, in a large mixing bowl, add together the lite mayonnaise, sour cream, apple cider vinegar, granulated sugar, and a pinch of ground black pepper. Whisk to combine.

7. Mix in the coleslaw mix, and season with fine salt, ground black pepper, and additional apple cider vinegar to taste. Serve the chicken breasts with coleslaw, and extra barbecue sauce if desired.

TOMATO TURKEY BALLS

COOK TIME: 14 MIN | SERVES: 2

INGREDIENTS:

- ½ cup whole-wheat orzo (risoni)
- 1 tbsp olive oil, plus extra for drizzling
- 1 tbsp garlic, crushed and divided
- 1 (8 oz) can tomato sauce
- ¾ cup water
- ¼ tsp ground black pepper, divided
- ⅛ tsp ground cumin
- 8 oz ground turkey
- ¾ cup zucchini, grated
- 1 tbsp thyme, minced, plus extra for serving
- ⅛ tsp sea salt
- ¼ cup crumbled herbed feta cheese

DIRECTIONS:

1. Preheat the air fryer to 400°F, or 200°C.

2. In a round, nonstick cake pan, mix the orzo, olive oil, and half of the crushed garlic, and spread into an even layer. Place the cake pan into the air-fryer basket, and the basket into the air fryer. Cook for 3 to 5 minutes, stirring half way through cooking, until the orzo is lightly browned and fragrant.

3. Mix the tomato sauce, water, ⅛ tsp ground black pepper, and ground cumin, into the orzo mixture until combined. Return the basket to the air fryer, and cook for 18 to 22 minutes, until the orzo is al dente.

4. In a medium-sized mixing bowl, combine the ground turkey, grated zucchini, minced thyme, sea salt, remaining crushed garlic, and the remaining ⅛ tsp ground black pepper. Use your hands to combine the ground turkey mixture, until it forms a cohesive mass. Using lightly moistened hands, divide the mixture into 8 portions, and roll into meatballs.

5. Stir the orzo mixture gently, and place the meatballs into it. Cook for 8 to 10 minutes, until the meatballs are lightly browned. Sprinkle the crumbled herbed feta cheese over the meatballs, and cook for 2 to 4 minutes, until the meatballs and feta are spotty brown.

6. Transfer the cake pan onto a wire rack, and allow the meatballs and orzo to rest for 5 minutes. Drizzle with extra olive oil, and sprinkle with extra thyme, before serving.

POULTRY

ASIAN SPICY WINGS

COOK TIME: 26 MIN | MAKES: 20

Ingredients:

For the sauce:
- 1 tbsp red pepper paste
- 2 tsp lite mayonnaise
- ½ tsp honey
- 2 tsp sesame oil
- 3 tbsp dark soy sauce
- 2 tsp garlic, minced
- 2 tsp light brown sugar
- 1 tsp ground ginger

For the wings:
- 1 lb. chicken wings, cut into drumettes and flats
- Olive oil cooking spray
- ½ tsp fine salt
- ½ tsp ground black pepper
- 1 tsp sesame seeds

Directions:

To make the sauce:

1. In a large mixing bowl, add together the red pepper paste, lite mayonnaise, honey, sesame oil, dark soy sauce, minced garlic, brown sugar, and ground ginger. Whisk to combine, and set aside.

To make the wings:

2. Preheat the air fryer to 400F, or 200°C.

3. Place the chicken wings in the fryer basket, spray with olive oil cooking spray, and sprinkle with fine salt and ground black pepper.

4. Bake for 10 minutes, then turn the wings, and spray with olive oil cooking spray. Cook for a further 10 minutes.

5. Remove the chicken wings, transfer to the large bowl with the sauce, and toss.

6. Return the coated wings to the fryer basket, and bake for 4 to 6 minutes, until the sauce has glazed, and the chicken is crisp. Serve warm, garnished with sesame seeds.

POULTRY

SERRANO CHICKEN WRAPS

COOK TIME: 12 MIN | SERVES: 2-4

Ingredients:

- 1 lb. boneless, skinless chicken breast
- 1 tsp olive oil
- 2 tbsp lemon juice
- 1 small onion, minced
- 1 tbsp oyster sauce, plus extra for serving
- 2 tsp light brown sugar
- ½ tbsp garlic, minced
- ⅛ tsp red pepper flakes
- 1 mango, peeled, pitted, and cut into pieces
- 1/3 cup mint, chopped
- 1/3 cup parsley, chopped
- 1/3 cup basil, chopped
- 1 head butter lettuce, leaves separated
- ¼ cup roasted peanuts, chopped
- 2 serrano peppers, seeds removed, thinly sliced

Directions:

1. Preheat the air fryer to 400°F, or 200°C.

2. Pat the chicken breasts dry with paper towels, and rub with olive oil. Place the chicken in the air-fryer basket, and place the basket the in air fryer. Cook for 12 to 16 minutes, flipping and rotating the chicken half way through cooking, until fully cooked.

3. In a large mixing bowl, add together the lemon juice, minced onion, oyster sauce, brown sugar, minced garlic, and red pepper flakes. Mix to combine, and set aside.

4. Place the chicken breasts on a cutting board, allow them to cool slightly, then shred them into bite-sized pieces. Add the shredded chicken breasts, mango pieces, chopped mint, chopped parsley, and chopped basil into the bowl with the dressing, and toss to coat. Serve the chicken mixture in the butter lettuce leaves, with chopped peanuts, sliced serrano peppers, and extra oyster sauce.

Tip: add some cucumber pieces to the wrap to balance out the serrano peppers.

POULTRY

CAYENNE TURKEY BREASTS

COOK TIME: 35 MIN | SERVES: 2

Ingredients:

- 1 tsp cayenne pepper
- ½ tsp fine salt
- ½ tsp ground black pepper
- 1 lb. broccoli florets, cut into pieces
- 1 onion, peeled and quartered
- 2 tbsp olive oil, divided
- 1½ tbsp lemon juice
- ½ tbsp garlic, minced
- 1-2 boneless turkey breasts, cut in half lengthwise
- 8 oz grape tomatoes, halved
- 1/3 cup parsley, chopped

Directions:

1. Preheat the air fryer to 400°F, or 200°C.

2. In a small mixing bowl, add together the cayenne pepper, fine salt, and ground black pepper, and mix to combine

3. In a large mixing bowl, combine the broccoli, quartered onion, 1 tbsp olive oil, and 1 tsp of the cayenne mixture. Transfer the vegetables to the air fryer basket, and spread into an even layer. In the same bowl, add together the lemon juice, minced garlic, 1 tsp of the cayenne mixture, and the remaining 1 tbsp olive oil. Mix to combine.

4. Using a metal skewer or toothpick, poke the turkey skin 10 to 15 times. Pat the turkey breasts dry with paper towels, and rub evenly with 1 tsp of the lemon juice mixture. Reserve any remaining lemon juice mixture for later.

5. Arrange the turkey, skin side up, on top of the vegetables, spaced evenly apart. Place the basket into the air fryer. Cook for 25 to 35 minutes, or until the vegetables are tender, and the turkey breasts are fully cooked and browned.

6. Transfer the breasts onto a plate, and allow them to rest for 5 minutes. Transfer the vegetables to the bowl with the remaining lemon juice mixture. Add the halved grape tomatoes and chopped parsley, and toss to coat. Season with fine salt and ground black pepper to taste. Serve the turkey breasts with the vegetables.

Tip: depending on the size of the turkey breast, you could cut one breast in half lengthwise, to make it into 2 turkey fillets.

POULTRY

CHEESY CHICKEN BUNS

COOK TIME: 12 MIN | SERVES: 2

Ingredients:

- ¼ cup plain breadcrumbs
- 2 tbsp Greek yogurt
- Fine salt
- Ground black pepper
- 8 oz ground chicken
- ¼ cup fiesta blend cheese, shredded
- 2 hamburger buns
- ½ beefsteak slicing tomato, thinly sliced
- 2 green leaf lettuce leaves

Directions:

1. Preheat the air fryer to 350°F, or 176°C.

2. In a large mixing bowl, combine the breadcrumbs, Greek yogurt, ¼ tsp fine salt, ¼ tsp ground black pepper, ground chicken, and the shredded fiesta blend cheese. Lightly knead with your hands, until the mixture forms a cohesive mass.

3. Divide the chicken mixture into 2 lightly packed balls, and gently flatten each ball into a thick patty. Press the center of each patty with your fingertips to make a deep depression. Season with fine salt and ground black pepper.

4. Arrange the chicken patties in the air fryer basket, spaced evenly apart. Place the basket in the air fryer, and cook for 12 to 16 minutes, flipping and rotating the burgers half way through cooking, until browned.

5. Transfer the patties onto the bottom halves of the buns, and top with sliced tomato and green leaf lettuce leaves.

Tip: you can top these burgers with homemade or store-bought guacamole.

TURKEY SAUSAGE ROAST

COOK TIME: 28 MIN | SERVES: 2

Ingredients:

- 1½ lb. sweet potatoes, peeled, and cut into pieces
- 4 tsp olive oil, divided, plus extra for drizzling
- ½ tsp rosemary, finely chopped
- ⅛ tsp sea salt
- ⅛ tsp smoked paprika
- 2 (6 oz) raw turkey sausages
- 2 tsp honey, warmed, divided
- 2 tsp apple cider vinegar
- 1 tsp whole-grain mustard
- ¼ tsp ground black pepper
- ½ small head red cabbage, cored and thinly sliced
- 2 tbsp pecan nuts, chopped
- 2 tbsp parsley, chopped

Directions:

1. Preheat the air fryer to 400°F, or 200°C.

2. In a medium-sized mixing bowl, combine the sweet potato pieces, 2 tsp olive oil, chopped rosemary, sea salt, and smoked paprika. Toss to coat. Place the seasoned sweet potatoes in the air fryer basket in an even layer. Place the basket into the air fryer, and cook for 10 to 15 minutes, until the potatoes are beginning to brown.

3. Coat each turkey sausage with 1 tsp warm honey. Mix the sweet potatoes, and arrange the turkey sausages on top, spaced evenly apart. Return the basket to the air fryer, and cook for 8 to 13 minutes, until the sweet potatoes are tender, and the sausages are lightly browned.

4. Transfer the sausages onto a plate, and allow to rest while finishing with the sweet potatoes.

5. In a large mixing bowl, add together the apple cider vinegar, whole-grain mustard, ground black pepper, remaining 2 tsp olive oil, and remaining 1 tsp honey. Whisk to combine.

6. Add the sweet potatoes, sliced red cabbage, chopped pecan nuts, and chopped parsley, and toss to coat. Season with sea salt and ground black pepper to taste. Serve the turkey sausages with the vegetables.

CHICKEN SCHNITZEL

COOK TIME: 8 MIN | SERVES: 4

Ingredients:

- 4 chicken breast cutlets
- Fine salt
- Ground black pepper
- 1 large egg, beaten
- ½ cup breadcrumbs
- 2 tbsp Romano cheese, grated
- Olive oil cooking spray
- 6 cups baby spinach
- 1 tbsp olive oil
- 1 tbsp lime juice, plus 1 lime cut into wedges for serving
- Shaved Romano cheese

Directions:

1. Preheat the air fryer to 400°F, or 200°C.

2. Place 1 chicken breast between two sheets of plastic wrap. Use a meat mallet or rolling pin to pound the breast until it is about ¼-inch thick. Repeat with the remaining chicken breasts. Season the chicken with ½ tsp fine salt, and ground black pepper to taste.

3. Place the beaten egg in a shallow, medium-sized bowl. In a separate bowl, add together the breadcrumbs and grated Romano cheese, and mix to combine. Dip the chicken breasts in the beaten egg, then in the breadcrumb mixture, until fully coated. Shake off any excess breadcrumbs, and place on a work surface. Spray both sides of the schnitzels with olive oil cooking spray.

4. Working in batches, place the coated chicken schnitzels in the air fryer basket. Cook for 8 minutes, flipping half way, until golden brown and fully cooked. Place the baby spinach in a large mixing bowl, and toss with olive oil, lime juice, ¼ tsp fine salt, and ground black pepper to taste.

5. Place a chicken schnitzel on each plate, and top with 1½ cups seasoned baby spinach. Serve with a lime wedge, and top with some shaved Romano cheese.

ITALIAN CHICKEN CUTLETS

COOK TIME: 10 MIN | SERVES: 4

INGREDIENTS:

For the chicken:
- 2 (8 oz) boneless, skinless chicken breasts
- ¼ tsp fine salt
- Ground black pepper
- Whites of 2 large eggs
- 2/3 cup breadcrumbs
- Olive oil cooking spray

For the sauce:
- 1 tbsp unsalted butter
- ½ cup reduced-sodium chicken stock
- ¼ cup dry white wine
- 1 lime, juiced, and lime halves reserved
- Ground black pepper
- 1 tbsp pitted black olives, chopped

For serving:
- 1 lime, sliced
- ¼ cup basil, chopped
- Parmesan cheese, grated

DIRECTIONS:

For the chicken:

1. Preheat the air fryer to 370°F, or 187°C.

2. Halve the chicken breasts horizontally to make 4 cutlets. Place the chicken cutlets between two sheets of plastic wrap. Use a rolling pin or meat mallet to pound the chicken cutlets to a ¼-inch thick. Season both sides of the chicken with fine salt and ground black pepper to taste.

3. In a medium-sized bowl, beat the egg whites with 1 tsp water. Place the breadcrumbs on a large plate. Dip the chicken, one cutlet at a time, in the beaten egg, then in the breadcrumbs. Place on a work surface. Generously spray both sides of the chicken cutlets with olive oil cooking spray.

4. Place the chicken cutlets in the air fryer. Cook for 6 minutes, flipping half way, until fully cooked, crisp, and golden.

For the sauce:

5. In a medium-sized saucepan, melt the unsalted butter over medium heat. Add the low-sodium chicken stock, white wine, lime juice, reserved lime halves, and ground black pepper to taste.

6. Boil over high heat for 3 to 4 minutes, until the liquid is reduced by half. Remove from the heat, discard the lime halves, and mix in the chopped black olives.

To serve:

7. Place the chicken cutlets on serving plates. Spoon 2 tbsp of the butter sauce over each chicken cutlet. Top with the lime slices, chopped basil and grated Parmesan cheese, and serve.

PEACH-COATED DRUMSTICKS

COOK TIME: 32 MIN | MAKES: 6

INGREDIENTS:

For the glaze:
- ½ cup peach preserves
- 2 tsp whole-grain mustard
- ¼ tsp chili powder
- ½ tsp dark soy sauce

For the drumsticks:
- Olive oil cooking spray
- 6 chicken drumsticks
- 1 tsp fine salt
- ½ tsp ground black pepper
- ½ tsp Cajun seasoning

DIRECTIONS:

To make the glaze:

1. In a small stock pot over low heat, add together the peach preserves, whole-grain mustard, chili powder, and dark soy sauce, whisk to combine.

2. Cook for 5 to 10 minutes, until slightly thickened.

3. Turn off the heat, and set aside.

To make the drumsticks:

4. Preheat the air fryer to 370°F, or 187°C.

5. Spray the drumsticks and the air fryer basket with olive oil cooking spray.

6. In a small mixing bowl, add together the fine salt, ground black pepper, and Cajun seasoning, and mix to combine.

7. Place the drumsticks in the air fryer basket, and sprinkle with half of the seasoning mixture. Bake for 10 minutes.

8. Remove the drumsticks, and flip. Spray with olive oil cooking spray, and sprinkle with the remaining seasoning mixture.

9. Place the drumsticks back in the air fryer, and bake for an additional 10 minutes.

10. Remove the drumsticks, and brush them with the peach glaze. Bake for 2 minutes, until the sauce is sticky and caramelized, and serve with your choice of side.

TURKEY POPS

COOK TIME: 15 MIN | MAKES: 3 CUPS

INGREDIENTS:

For the sauce:
- ¼ cup whole-grain mustard
- ½ tsp Worcestershire sauce
- ½ tsp garlic, crushed
- 1 tsp apple cider vinegar
- ½ tsp light brown sugar
- ⅛ tsp ground black pepper
- ¼ teaspoon chili powder
- ¼ tsp onion powder

For the turkey:
- 3 cups panko breadcrumbs
- ½ tsp garlic powder
- ½ tsp crushed red pepper flakes
- ¼ tsp cayenne pepper
- ¼ tsp ground black pepper
- ½ cup cornstarch
- 1 cup whole milk
- Olive oil cooking spray
- 2 to 3 boneless, skinless turkey breasts, cut into cubes

DIRECTIONS:

To make the sauce:

1. In a small mixing bowl, add together the whole-grain mustard, Worcestershire sauce, crushed garlic, apple cider vinegar, brown sugar, ground black pepper, chili powder, and onion powder. Whisk to combine, and refrigerate until ready to use.

To make the turkey:

2. Preheat the air fryer to 400°F, or 200°C. Spray the air fryer basket with olive oil cooking spray.

3. Place the panko breadcrumbs into a large mixing bowl, and add the garlic powder, crushed red pepper flakes, cayenne pepper, and ground black pepper. Mix to combine.

4. Put the cornstarch and whole milk in a separate medium-sized mixing bowl.

5. Dip the cubed turkey in the cornstarch, then in the whole milk, and then in the panko breadcrumb mixture.

6. Working in batches, place the crumbed turkey cubes in a single layer in the prepared air fryer basket.

7. Spray the top of the turkey with olive oil cooking spray.

8. Fry for 10 minutes, flip the turkey cubes, and spray again with olive oil cooking spray. Continue to fry for an additional 5 minutes, or until the turkey cubes are fully cooked and golden brown.

9. Serve with the whole-grain mustard sauce on the side.

MARINARA CHICKEN BALLS

COOK TIME: 12 MIN | SERVES: 4

Ingredients:

- 1 lb. ground chicken
- 1 large egg
- ¼ tsp crushed red pepper flakes
- ¼ cup breadcrumbs
- 1 tsp fine salt
- ½ tsp garlic, crushed
- ½ tsp onion powder
- ½ tsp ground black pepper
- 24 oz jar Italian herbs and garlic marinara sauce

Directions:

1. Preheat the air fryer to 360°F, or 182°C.

2. In a large mixing bowl, add together the ground chicken, large egg, crushed red pepper flakes, breadcrumbs, fine salt, crushed garlic, onion powder, and ground black pepper. Mix to combine.

3. Roll the chicken mixture into 12 balls, and place them into the air fryer basket, spaced apart.

4. Cook for 10 to 12 minutes, or until the chicken balls are cooked through and browned.

5. While the chicken meatballs are cooking, pour the jar of marinara sauce into a medium-sized stockpot, and stir until heated through.

6. Serve the chicken meatballs with your choice of pasta, and spoon over the marinara sauce.

POULTRY

SWEET CHICKEN SKEWERS

COOK TIME: 10 MIN | MAKES: 4

Ingredients:

For the glaze:
- 1/3 cup honey
- 1/3 cup sweet soy sauce
- ½ tsp sea salt
- ½ tsp ground black pepper

For the kebabs:
- 1 green bell pepper, seeds removed, cut into chunks
- 6 small white mushrooms, cut in half
- ½ cup pineapple chunks
- 4 boneless, skinless chicken breasts
- 4-8 wooden skewers, soaked in water
- Olive oil cooking spray
- ¼ tsp sesame seeds

Directions:

To make the glaze:

1. In a small mixing bowl, add together the honey, sweet soy sauce, fine salt, and ground black pepper. Mix to combine, and set aside.

To make the kebabs:

2. Preheat the air fryer to 380°F, or 193°C.

3. Place the green pepper chunks, halved mushrooms, and pineapple chunks in their own small bowls.

4. Cut the chicken breasts into cubes.

5. Using wooden skewers that will fit in your air fryer, assemble the skewers by alternating colors and ingredients, until each skewer is full.

6. Place in the air fryer basket, and spray with olive oil cooking spray.

7. Roast for 8 minutes, or until the chicken is fully cooked.

8. Brush the sweet soy sauce glaze over the cooked chicken skewers, and roast for another 1 to 2 minutes, or until the sauce is sticky and caramelized.

9. Garnish with sesame seeds before serving.

POULTRY

HERBED HEN ROAST

COOK TIME: 45 MIN | SERVES: 2

Ingredients:

- 1 (1½- to 2 lb.) Rock Cornish game hen
- ¼ cup sunflower oil
- 2 tbsp lime juice
- 2 tbsp rosemary, chopped
- 2 tbsp oregano, chopped
- 2 tbsp garlic, crushed
- 1 tsp fine salt
- 1 tsp ground black pepper
- 1 leek, roughly chopped
- ½ small red onion
- ½ lime
- Chopped cilantro, for garnish
- Ground black pepper, for garnish

Directions:

1. Preheat the air fryer to 380°F, or 193°C.

2. In a small mixing bowl, add together the sunflower oil, lime juice, chopped rosemary, chopped oregano, crushed garlic, fine salt, and ground black pepper. Mix to combine. Brush the herb mixture all over the hen. Pour any excess herb mixture into the cavity of the bird.

3. Stuff the chopped leek, red onion, and ½ lime into the cavity of the hen.

4. Place the hen inside the air fryer basket, and roast for 40 to 45 minutes, or until fully cooked, and the juices run clear.

5. Cut the Cornish hen in half, and serve with a sprinkle of chopped cilantro and ground black pepper.

Tip: you can choose any ingredients that you want to stuff the Cornish hen with.

POULTRY

CHICKEN PARMESAN

COOK TIME: 8 MIN | SERVES: 4

Ingredients:

- 4 boneless, skinless chicken breasts
- Fine salt
- Ground black pepper
- 1 large egg, beaten
- ½ cup panko breadcrumbs
- 2 tbsp Parmesan cheese, grated
- Olive oil cooking spray
- 6 cups mixed salad greens
- 1 tbsp olive oil
- 1 tbsp lime juice, plus 1 lime cut into wedges for serving
- Shaved Parmesan cheese

Directions:

1. Preheat the air fryer to 400°F, or 200°C.

2. Place a chicken breast between two sheets of plastic wrap. Use a meat mallet or rolling pin to pound to a ¼-inch thick. Season the breast with ½ tsp fine salt, and ground black pepper to taste. Repeat with the remaining breasts.

3. Place the beaten egg in a shallow, medium-sized bowl. In a separate bowl, add the panko breadcrumbs and grated Parmesan cheese together, and mix to combine.

4. Dip the chicken breasts in the beaten egg, then in the breadcrumb mixture. Place on a work surface, and spray both sides with olive oil cooking spray.

5. Place the crumbed chicken breasts in the air fryer basket. Cook for 8 minutes, flipping half way, until golden brown and fully cooked.

6. Place the mixed greens in a bowl, and toss with the olive oil, lime juice, ¼ tsp fine salt, and ground black pepper to taste.

7. Place each crumbed chicken breast on a plate, and top with 1½ cups mixed greens salad. Serve with lime wedges, and top with some shaved Parmesan.

BEEF, LAMB, & PORK

DIJON ROAST PORK

COOK TIME: 35 MIN | SERVES: 8

INGREDIENTS:

For the pork:
- 1 (2 lb.) boneless pork shoulder roast, at room temperature
- 1 tsp fine salt
- 1 tsp olive oil
- 1 tbsp Dijon mustard
- ½ tbsp garlic, minced

Greek yogurt and chives dip:
- 2/3 cup Greek yogurt
- 2¼ tbsp Dijon mustard
- 2 tbsp chives, chopped
- ¼ tsp fine salt
- Ground black pepper

DIRECTIONS:

For the pork:

1. Preheat the air fryer to 325°F, or 162°C.

2. Pat the pork shoulder dry with paper towels, and season with fine salt.

3. In a small mixing bowl, add together the olive oil, Dijon mustard, and minced garlic, and mix to combine. Rub the outside of the pork roast with the mustard mixture.

4. Place the pork in the air fryer basket. Cook for 30 to 35 minutes, flipping half way, until browned and cooked through.

For the dip:

1. In a medium-sized mixing bowl, combine the Greek yogurt, Dijon mustard, chopped chives, fine salt, and ground black pepper to taste. Mix until smooth, and refrigerate until ready to use.

2. Transfer the pork roast to a cutting board, and allow to rest for 10 to 15 minutes before carving. Thinly slice the pork roast, and serve with the Greek yogurt and chives dip on the side.

BEEF, LAMB, & PORK

HONEY & MUSTARD CHOPS

COOK TIME: 24 MIN | SERVES: 2

Ingredients:

- 1 lb. carrots, peeled, and cut into sticks
- 4 tsp sunflower oil
- Fine salt
- Ground black pepper
- 1 tbsp honey, warmed
- 4 (6 oz) lamb shoulder chops
- 1 tbsp whole-grain mustard
- 1½ tsp rosemary, chopped
- ½ tbsp garlic, crushed
- 1 tsp lime zest plus 1 tsp lime juice
- 1 tsp water

Directions:

1. Preheat the air fryer to 350°F, or 176°C.

2. In a medium-sized mixing bowl, combine the carrot sticks, 1 tsp sunflower oil, ⅛ tsp fine salt, and ⅛ tsp ground black pepper, Toss to coat. Transfer the carrots to the air-fryer basket. Place the basket in the air fryer, and cook for 14 minutes, stirring half way through cooking.

3. In a small mixing bowl, add together the 2 tsp warmed honey and 2 tsp sunflower oil, and whisk to combine. Pat the lamb chops dry with paper towels, brush with the honey-oil mixture, and season with fine salt and ground black pepper.

4. Stir the carrots, and place the lamb chops on top, spaced evenly apart. Return the basket to the air fryer, and cook for 10 to 15 minutes, flipping and rotating the chops half way through cooking, until they are lightly browned and fully cooked.

5. In a medium-sized, microwave-safe bowl, add together the whole-grain mustard, chopped rosemary, crushed garlic, lime zest, and lime juice, water, 1 tsp sunflower oil, and the remaining 1 tsp honey. Whisk to combine, and microwave for 30 seconds, until fragrant. Transfer the lamb chops to a plate, and brush with 1 tbsp of the whole-grain mustard mixture.

6. Transfer the carrots to the bowl with the remaining whole-grain mustard mixture, and toss to coat. Season with fine salt and ground black pepper to taste. Serve the lamb with the carrots.

BEEF, LAMB, & PORK

ROSEMARY BEEF ROAST

COOK TIME: 40 MIN | SERVES: 6-8

Ingredients:

- 1 (3 lb.) beef chuck tender roast, at room temperature
- Olive oil cooking spray
- 1 tsp garlic powder
- 1 tsp onion powder
- 2 tsp rosemary, finely chopped
- 1 tsp fine salt
- ½ tsp ground black pepper

Directions:

1. Preheat the air fryer to 360°F, or 182°C.

2. Pat the beef roast dry with paper towels.

3. Spray the beef roast with olive oil cooking spray until well coated. In a small mixing bowl, add together the garlic powder, onion powder, chopped rosemary, fine salt, and ground black pepper. Mix to combine, and season the beef roast with half of the seasoning mixture.

4. Place the roast in the air fryer basket, and roast for 25 minutes.

5. Flip the beef roast over, and spray with olive oil cooking spray. Sprinkle on the remaining seasoning mixture.

6. Return the beef to the air fryer, and bake for an additional 15 minutes, or until browned, and cooked to your desired consistency.

7. Remove the beef roast from the air fryer, and allow to rest for 10 minutes before slicing, and serving with your choice of side.

Tip: cut the beef roast in half if it is too big to fit inside the air fryer basket.

HONEY HICKORY RIBS

COOK TIME: 18 MIN | SERVES: 4

Ingredients:

- 2 tsp smoked paprika
- 2 tsp light brown sugar
- 2 tbsp honey hickory rub
- Fine salt
- Ground black pepper
- 1½ lb. boneless short ribs
- 2 tsp plus 2 tbsp olive oil
- ¼ cup red bell pepper, finely chopped
- 1 small red onion, finely chopped
- 1 tbsp garlic, minced
- Pinch crushed red pepper flakes
- 2 tbsp parsley, finely chopped
- 2 tsp lime juice

Directions:

1. Preheat the air fryer to 250°F, or 120°C.

2. In a small mixing bowl, add together the smoked paprika, light brown sugar, honey hickory rub, ½ tsp fine salt, and ¼ tsp ground black pepper. Mix to combine.

3. Pat the short ribs dry with paper towels, rub with 2 tsp olive oil, and sprinkle evenly with the seasoning mixture. Place the seasoned short ribs in the air-fryer basket, spaced evenly apart. Place the basket in the air fryer, and cook for 18 to 24 minutes, flipping the short ribs half way through, until fully cooked. Transfer the short ribs to a cutting board, and allow to rest.

4. In a microwave-safe bowl, combine the chopped red bell pepper, finely chopped onion, minced garlic, crushed red pepper flakes, ⅛ tsp fine salt, and remaining 2 tbsp olive oil. Microwave for 2 minutes, stirring occasionally, until the vegetables have softened. Allow to cool slightly, then stir in the chopped parsley and lime juice. Season with fine salt and ground black pepper to taste. Slice the short ribs thinly, and serve with the red bell pepper relish.

BEEF, LAMB, & PORK

TZATZIKI PORK PITAS

COOK TIME: 14 MIN | SERVES: 2

Ingredients:

- 1 tbsp sunflower oil
- 1 ½ tbsp garlic, minced, divided
- 1 tsp dried thyme
- 1 tsp ground cumin
- 1 tsp smoked paprika
- ½ tsp sea salt, divided
- ½ tsp ground black pepper, divided
- 8 oz boneless pork ribs
- Aluminum foil
- 1 cucumber, half shredded, and the other half thinly sliced
- 6 tbsp plain Greek yogurt
- 1 tbsp lime juice, divided, plus lime wedges for serving
- 1 tsp dill, chopped
- 2 (8-inch) pitas
- 1 cup baby spinach
- 1 small red onion, halved and thinly sliced

Directions:

1. Preheat the air fryer to 400°F, or 200°C.

2. In a medium-sized, microwave-safe bowl, add together the sunflower oil, ½ tbsp minced garlic, dried thyme, ground cumin, smoked paprika, ¼ tsp sea salt, and ¼ tsp ground black pepper. Mix to combine, and microwave for 30 seconds, until fragrant.

3. Rub the pork ribs with half of the seasoning oil mixture, and place them in the air-fryer basket, spaced evenly apart. Place the basket into the air fryer, and cook for 6 to 10 minutes, flipping the ribs half way, until they are lightly browned. Transfer the ribs to a cutting board, tent with aluminum foil, and allow them to rest for 5 minutes.

4. In a medium-sized mixing bowl, add together the shredded cucumber, Greek yogurt, 1 tsp lime juice, chopped dill, remaining 1 tbsp minced garlic, remaining ¼ tsp sea salt, and remaining ¼ tsp ground black pepper. Mix to combine.

5. Wrap the pitas tightly in aluminum foil, and place them in the empty air fryer basket. Return the basket to the air fryer, and cook for 2 to 4 minutes, until the pitas are heated through.

6. In a medium-sized mixing bowl, add together the remaining 2 tsp lime juice, and the remaining seasoning oil mixture. Whisk to combine.

7. Slice the pork ribs thinly, and add them to the lime-oil mixture. Toss to coat. Divide the pork evenly between the warmed pitas, and top with tzatziki sauce, sliced cucumber, baby spinach, and sliced red onion. Serve with lime wedges.

BEEF, LAMB, & PORK

HONEY NY STRIP

COOK TIME: 22 MIN | SERVES: 2

Ingredients:

- 1 lb. russet potatoes, peeled and cubed
- 3 tbsp sunflower oil
- Fine salt
- Ground black pepper
- 4 tsp honey, warmed, plus extra for drizzling
- 2 (4 oz) New York strip steaks
- Aluminum foil
- 2 tbsp cilantro, chopped
- 1½ tsp apple cider vinegar
- ½ tsp dried oregano
- ½ tbsp garlic, crushed
- ⅛ tsp crushed red pepper flakes

Directions:

1. Preheat the air fryer to 400°F, or 200°C.

2. In a medium-sized mixing bowl, add together the cubed potatoes, 2 tsp sunflower oil, ¼ tsp fine salt, and ¼ tsp ground black pepper. Toss to combine. Place the potatoes into the air fryer basket, and cook for 12 minutes.

3. In a small mixing bowl, add together the warmed honey and 1 tsp sunflower oil, and whisk to combine. Pat the steaks dry with paper towels, brush with the honey-oil mixture, and season with fine salt and ground black pepper.

4. Place the steaks on top of the potatoes, spaced evenly apart. Return the basket to the air fryer, and cook for 8 to 10 minutes, flipping and rotating the steaks half way through, until they are browned, and fully cooked. Transfer the steaks onto a cutting board, and the potatoes to a serving bowl. Tent each with aluminum foil, and allow to rest until serving.

5. In a small mixing bowl, add together the remaining 2 tbsp oil, chopped cilantro, apple cider vinegar, dried oregano, crushed garlic, crushed red pepper flakes, and fine salt and ground black pepper to taste. Mix to combine. Cut the steaks into thin strips, and serve with the potatoes, oil-vinegar dressing, and a drizzle of honey.

BEEF, LAMB, & PORK

HAWAIIAN BEEF SANDWICH

COOK TIME: 7 MIN | MAKES: 6

Ingredients:

- 6 Hawaiian sweet rolls
- ½ lb. cooked roast beef, sliced
- ½ cup crispy fried onions
- 6 cheddar cheese slices
- 6 pineapple slices
- 2 tbsp unsalted butter, melted
- ½ tsp onion powder
- ¼ tsp garlic powder
- 1 tbsp black sesame seeds

Directions:

1. Preheat the air fryer to 350°F, or 176°C. Line the air fryer basket with parchment liner.

2. Cut the Hawaiian rolls in half to create slider buns, and place 6 halves in the air fryer basket.

3. Top the half buns with the cooked roast beef slices, crispy fried onions, and cheddar cheese slices.

4. Bake for 5 minutes without the top halves of the rolls, until the cheese is melted.

5. Place the pineapple slices on top of the melted cheese, and place the top halves of the rolls on top of the pineapple slices. Brush the tops of the rolls with the melted butter.

6. Sprinkle the tops of each bun with the onion powder, garlic powder, and black sesame seeds, and bake for another 2 minutes. Serve immediately.

BEEF, LAMB, & PORK

JAPANESE MISO STEAK

COOK TIME: 38 MIN | SERVES: 2

Ingredients:

- 12 oz shiitake mushrooms, stemmed, and cut in half
- 2 spring onions, white and green parts separated, and thinly sliced
- 2 tbsp sesame oil, divided
- ½ tsp sea salt, divided
- 2 zucchinis, halved lengthwise
- 1-2 (8 to 12 oz) ribeye steaks
- 1 tbsp sunflower oil, divided
- Aluminum foil
- 1 tbsp white miso
- 1 tbsp warm water
- 1 tbsp rice vinegar
- ½ tbsp garlic, minced
- ¼ tsp ground black pepper

Directions:

1. Preheat the air fryer to 400°F, or 200°C.

2. In a large mixing bowl, add together the shiitake mushrooms, sliced spring onion whites, 1 tsp sesame oil, and ⅛ tsp sea salt. Mix to combine. Place the mushroom mixture in the air fryer basket. In the same bowl, combine the halved zucchinis, 1 tsp sesame oil, and ⅛ tsp sea salt, and toss to coat. Arrange the zucchinis, cut sides up, on top of the mushroom mixture, spaced evenly apart.

3. Place the basket into the air fryer, and cook for 15 to 20 minutes, until the vegetables have softened and lightly browned. Transfer the zucchinis to a cutting board, and the mushroom mixture to an empty bowl. Cover to keep warm.

4. Pat the ribeye steaks dry with paper towels, rub with 1 tsp sunflower oil, and sprinkle with the remaining ¼ tsp sea salt.

5. Place the steaks in the empty air fryer basket, and return the basket to the air fryer. Cook for 12 to 18 minutes, flipping and rotating the steaks half way through, until they are lightly browned. Transfer the steaks to the cutting board with the zucchinis, tent with aluminum foil, and allow to rest for 5 minutes.

6. In a small mixing bowl, combine the white miso and warm water, and whisk until the miso has dissolved. Add the rice vinegar, minced garlic, ground black pepper, remaining 1 tsp sesame oil, and remaining 2 tsp sunflower oil. Whisk to combine.

7. Cut the zucchinis into thick pieces. Add the zucchinis, the sliced green parts of the spring onions, and 1 tbsp of the miso dressing to the bowl with the mushroom mixture, and toss to combine. Season with sea salt and ground black pepper to taste. Slice the ribeye steaks thinly, and serve with the mushroom and zucchini mixture, drizzling over the remaining dressing.

BEEF, LAMB, & PORK

CUMIN LAMB CHOPS

COOK TIME: 15 MIN | Serves: 4

INGREDIENTS:

Cumin and dill rub:
- 2 tsp dried dill
- 1 tsp olive oil
- ½ tsp ground cumin
- ¼ tsp granulated sugar
- ⅛ tsp sea salt
- ⅛ tsp ground black pepper
- ½ tsp smoked paprika

Lamb chops:
- 4 lamb loin chops
- Aluminum foil

DIRECTIONS:

Cumin and dill rub:

1. In a small mixing bowl, add together the dried dill, olive oil, ground cumin, granulated sugar, sea salt, ground black pepper, and smoked paprika. Mix to combine.

For the lamb chops:

1. Preheat the air fryer to 400°F, or 200°C.

2. Dry the lamb chops with paper towels. Rub each lamb chop with the spice rub mixture. Place the lamb chops in the air fryer basket, and place the basket into the air fryer.

3. Cook for 10 to 15 minutes, flipping the chops half way through, until they are lightly browned. Transfer the chops onto a plate, tent with aluminum foil, and allow to rest for 5 minutes before serving.

SAUSAGE-STUFFED PEPPERS

COOK TIME: 25 MIN | SERVES: 4

Ingredients:

- 5 links of sweet Italian sausage
- 4 medium red bell peppers, halved lengthwise, and seeds removed
- Olive oil cooking spray
- 1 cup traditional marinara sauce
- 1½ cups (6 oz) mozzarella cheese, shredded
- 12 pepperoni slices, halved

Directions:

1. Preheat the air fryer to 370°F, or 187°C.

2. Place the Italian sausages in the air fryer basket, and cook for 10 minutes, flipping half way, until cooked through. Set aside to cool, then chop into small pieces.

3. Spray both sides of the red bell peppers with olive oil cooking spray.

4. Reduce the air fryer temperature to 350°F, or 176°C.

5. Place the red bell peppers in the air fryer basket, and cook for 6 to 8 minutes, flipping half way, until slightly softened. Transfer onto a plate.

6. In a medium-sized mixing bowl, add together the marinara sauce, shredded mozzarella, the chopped Italian sausage, and the halved pepperoni. Mix to combine. Fill each red bell pepper half with the cheese and sausage mixture.

7. Working in batches, place the stuffed bell peppers in a single layer in the air fryer. Cook for 6 to 7 minutes, until the cheese has melted, and the sauce is hot. Serve immediately.

BEEF STEW FRY

COOK TIME: 13 MIN | MAKES: 4 CUPS

Ingredients:

For the marinade:
- 2 tbsp water
- 3 tbsp hoisin sauce
- 3 tsp Worcestershire sauce
- 1 tsp garlic, crushed
- 1 tsp onion powder
- 1 tsp sesame oil
- ½ tsp ground ginger
- ½ tsp ground black pepper

For the beef:
- ½ lb. beef lean stew meat
- 1 cup cauliflower florets
- 1 green bell pepper, seeds removed, cut into strips
- 1 yellow bell pepper, seeds removed, cut into strips
- ¼ red onion, sliced
- ¼ shallot, sliced
- 2 tbsp sesame oil

Directions:

To make the marinade:

1. In a small mixing bowl, add together the water, hoisin sauce, Worcestershire sauce, crushed garlic, onion powder, sesame oil, ground ginger, and ground black pepper. Whisk to combine.

To make the beef:

1. Preheat the air fryer to 200°F, or 93°C.

2. Place the stewing beef in a large, zip-top bag, and add the marinade. Close the bag, refrigerate, and allow to marinate for 20 minutes.

3. In a medium-sized mixing bowl, combine the cauliflower florets, green bell pepper slices, yellow bell pepper slices, red onion slices, shallot slices, and sesame oil. Toss to coat.

4. Transfer the coated vegetables to the air fryer basket, and grill for 7 minutes, mixing half way through cooking, until softened and slightly charred.

5. Transfer the cooked vegetables to a large mixing bowl. Turn the heat up on the air fryer, to 360°F, or 182°C.

6. Remove the stewing beef from the marinade. Place the beef in the air fryer basket, and grill for 6 minutes, mixing half way, until browned and slightly charred.

7. Transfer the beef to the large bowl with the vegetables, toss to coat, and serve.

CHINESE PORK CHOPS

COOK TIME: 12 MIN | SERVES: 4

Ingredients:

- 8 boneless pork loin chops
- 1½ tbsp garlic, minced
- ¼ cup low-sodium soy sauce
- ½ tsp Chinese five-spice powder
- 3 tbsp honey
- 1 tbsp light brown sugar
- ¼ tsp crushed red pepper flakes
- 2 spring onions, chopped

Directions:

1. In a large mixing bowl, combine the pork chops, minced garlic, soy sauce, Chinese five-spice, and honey. Toss to coat. Cover, and allow to marinate in the refrigerator for 2 hours, or overnight.

2. Preheat the air fryer to 400°F, or 200°C.

3. Arrange the pork chops in a single layer in the air fryer basket, and cook for 5 minutes. Flip the pork chops, brush the tops with the marinade, and sprinkle with light brown sugar and crushed red pepper flakes.

4. Continue cooking for 4 to 6 minutes, until the tops are browned and caramelized. Top with the chopped spring onions, and serve.

BEEF, LAMB, & PORK

GROUND BEEF LOAF

COOK TIME: 25 MIN | SERVES: 6

INGREDIENTS:

- 1 lb. lean ground beef
- 2 large eggs
- 2 beefsteak tomatoes, diced
- ½ red onion, diced
- ½ cup plain breadcrumbs
- 1 tsp garlic powder
- 1 tsp dried marjoram
- 1 tsp dried thyme
- 1 tsp fine salt
- 1 tsp ground black pepper
- 3 oz cheddar cheese, shredded
- 2 tbsp olive oil
- Chopped cilantro, for garnish

DIRECTIONS:

1. Preheat the oven to 380°F, or 193°C.

2. In a large mixing bowl, add together the ground beef, large eggs, diced tomatoes, diced onion, breadcrumbs, garlic powder, dried marjoram, dried thyme, fine salt, ground black pepper, and shredded cheddar cheese. Mix to combine.

3. Form the ground beef mixture into a loaf, flattening to 1-inch thick.

4. Brush the top of the beef loaf with olive oil, then place the meatloaf into the air fryer basket, and cook for 25 minutes, until browned.

5. Remove from the air fryer, and allow to rest for 5 minutes before slicing, and serving with a sprinkle of chopped cilantro.

Ingredient tip: This recipe can be made using any kind of ground meat, like turkey, chicken, pork, or lamb.

MEDITERRANEAN LAMB OVALS

COOK TIME: 10 MIN | SERVES: 6

Ingredients:

For the lamb:
- 1 lb. ground lamb
- ¼ cup cilantro, roughly chopped
- 1 tbsp garlic, minced
- ¼ yellow onion, diced
- 1 tsp fine salt
- 1 tsp ground coriander
- ½ tsp ground black pepper
- ¼ tsp ground allspice
- ¼ tsp smoked paprika
- ¼ tsp ground ginger
- 3 tbsp olive oil, divided

For the mint and olive sauce:
- 1 cup plain Greek yogurt
- ½ cup mint, chopped
- ½ tbsp garlic, minced
- 2 tbsp lime juice
- ½ tsp ground coriander
- ¼ tsp smoked paprika
- ¼ tsp fine salt
- ¼ tsp ground black pepper
- 1 tbsp olive paste

Directions:

To make the lamb:

1. Preheat the air fryer to 360°F, or 182°C.

2. In a large mixing bowl, add together the ground lamb, chopped cilantro, minced garlic, diced onion, fine salt, ground coriander, ground black pepper, ground allspice, smoked paprika, ground ginger, and 2 tbsp olive oil. Mix to combine.

3. Divide the lamb mixture into 4 equal portions, and roll each portion into a long oval, by hand.

4. Brush the remaining 1 tbsp of olive oil over the lamb ovals, place them in an even layer in the air fryer basket, and cook for 10 minutes, or until fully cooked.

To make the mint and olive sauce:

1. In a small mixing bowl, add together the Greek yogurt, chopped mint, minced garlic, lime juice, ground coriander, smoked paprika, fine salt, ground black pepper, and olive paste. Mix to combine, and set aside.

2. Serve each lamb oval with a generous helping of mint and olive sauce for dipping.

VEGETABLE & PORK SKEWERS

COOK TIME: 18 MIN | SERVES: 2

Ingredients:

- 2 tbsp vegetable oil
- 1 tsp ginger, grated
- ½ tbsp garlic, minced
- ¼ tsp cayenne pepper
- 2 tbsp sesame oil
- 2 tsp dark soy sauce
- 2 tsp honey
- 1 tsp grated orange zest, plus 1 tbsp juice
- 4 boneless pork loin chops, cut into cubes
- 1 small yellow onion, halved, and cut into 6 equal wedges
- 4 oz white mushrooms, halved
- 1 large zucchini, sliced into rounds
- ¼ tsp fine salt
- ¼ tsp ground black pepper
- 6 (6-inch) wooden skewers, soaked in water

Directions:

1. Preheat the air fryer to 400°F, or 200°C.

2. In a large, microwave-safe bowl, add together 4 tsp vegetable oil, grated ginger, minced garlic, and cayenne pepper. Mix to combine, and microwave for 30 seconds, until fragrant. Add the sesame oil, dark soy sauce, honey, orange zest, and orange juice, and whisk to combine. Reserve 3 tbsp of the oil mixture. Add the cubed pork chops to the remaining oil mixture, and toss to coat. Set aside.

3. In a medium-sized bowl, combine the onion wedges, halved mushrooms, zucchini rounds, the remaining 2 tsp vegetable oil, fine salt, and ground black pepper. Toss to coat.

4. Assemble the skewers by threading 1 onion wedge first, followed by the zucchini and halved mushrooms. Repeat this for the remaining skewers and vegetables.

5. Arrange the skewers in the air fryer basket, spaced evenly apart. Place the basket in the air fryer, and cook for 8 minutes, or until the vegetables are beginning to brown.

6. Thread the pork pieces evenly onto the remaining 2 skewers. Flip and rotate the vegetable skewers, then arrange the pork skewers on top. Return the basket to the air fryer, and cook for 10 to 14 minutes, flipping the skewers half way, until the pork is fully cooked, and the vegetables are tender.

7. Whisk the reserved oil mixture to recombine. Using a fork, push the pork and vegetables off the skewers, and onto a platter. Drizzle with the oil mixture, and serve.

VEGETARIAN MAINS

VEGETARIAN MAINS

ROASTED CARROTS WITH NUTS

COOK TIME: 18 MIN | SERVES: 2

Ingredients:

- 4 carrots, peeled, and cut into quarters lengthwise
- 4 tsp sunflower oil, divided
- ¼ tsp sea salt, divided
- ½ cup boiling water
- 1½ tsp balsamic vinegar
- ⅛ tsp ground black pepper
- 1 tbsp mixed nuts, chopped
- 1 tbsp dried berries and golden raisins mix

Directions:

1. Preheat the air fryer to 375°F, or 190°C.

2. In a large mixing bowl, combine the cut carrots, 1 tsp sunflower oil, and ⅛ tsp sea salt, and toss to coat.

3. Pour the boiling water into the bottom of air the fryer basket, then arrange the carrots in the basket, and cook for 14 to 18 minutes, flipping half way, until the carrots are browned, and fully cooked.

4. Transfer the carrots to a serving platter, and season with sea salt and ground black pepper to taste.

5. In a small mixing bowl, add together the balsamic vinegar, ground black pepper, remaining 1 tbsp sunflower oil, and remaining ⅛ tsp sea salt. Whisk to combine.

6. Drizzle the balsamic vinaigrette over the carrots, and sprinkle with chopped mixed nuts, and the dried berries mix. Serve warm, or at room temperature.

VEGETARIAN MAINS

LEGUME BURGERS

COOK TIME: 6 MIN | MAKES: 6

Ingredients:

- Canola oil cooking spray
- 8 oz white mushrooms, trimmed and quartered
- ½ cup pine nuts
- 1 small red onion, quartered
- ½ cup cooked couscous,
- ¼ cup water
- 3 tbsp sunflower oil
- ½ tsp sea salt
- 1 (15 oz) can brown lentils, rinsed
- ½ cup panko breadcrumbs
- 1-6 cheddar cheese slices
- 1-6 hamburger buns

Directions:

1. Preheat the air fryer to 400°F, or 200°C. Spray the air fryer basket with canola oil cooking spray.

2. In a food processor, pulse the white mushrooms, pine nuts, and red onion until finely chopped. Transfer the vegetables to a large, microwave-safe bowl, and add the cooked couscous, water, sunflower oil, and sea salt. Mix to combine.

3. Microwave for 6 minutes, stirring occasionally, until most of the liquid has been absorbed. Allow to cool slightly.

4. Mix the brown lentils and the breadcrumbs into the vegetable-couscous mixture, until the mixture is combined, and forms a cohesive mass.

5. Using lightly-moistened hands, divide the mixture into 6 equal portions. Then tightly pack each portion into a thick patty.

6. Space the patties in the prepared basket, and place the basket into the air fryer. Cook for 10 to 15 minutes, until the patties are golden brown, and crisp. Turn off the air fryer.

7. Top each patty with 1 slice of cheddar cheese, and let the patties sit in the warm air fryer until the cheese is melted. Transfer the patties to a plate.

8. Place the top and bottom buns, cut side up, in the now-empty basket. Return the basket to the air fryer, and cook for 4 to 6 minutes, until the buns are lightly toasted. Serve the patties on the buns.

Tip: Make a homemade guacamole, and place it on top of the patties before placing the top bun on each burger.

VEGETARIAN MAINS

GARBANZO FRITTERS

COOK TIME: 12 MIN | SERVES: 2

INGREDIENTS:

- 1 (16 oz) can garbanzo beans, drained and rinsed
- ½ cup shallots, thinly sliced, and divided
- 1/3 cup parsley, finely chopped
- 2 tbsp lime juice
- 1 tsp garlic, crushed
- 1 tsp ground coriander
- ¼ cup garbanzo flour
- 6 cups iceberg lettuce, chopped
- 1 cup grape tomatoes, halved
- 1 medium cucumber, cut into thin rounds
- ¼ cup Lemon-Tahini Dressing

DIRECTIONS:

1. Preheat the air fryer to 375°F, or 190°C.

2. In a medium-sized mixing bowl, mash the garbanzo beans with a fork. Add ¼ cup sliced shallots, and the chopped parsley, lime juice, crushed garlic, ground coriander, and garbanzo flour. Mix to combine.

3. Use wet hands to shape the mixture into 8 equal patty shapes.

4. Place the patties in the air fryer basket, and bake for 12 minutes, flipping them half way, until lightly browned.

5. In a large mixing bowl, add together the chopped iceberg lettuce, halved tomatoes, cucumber rounds, and remaining ¼ cup of shallots. Toss to combine.

6. Allow the fritters to cool slightly before adding them to the tossed salad. Pour the lemon-tahini dressing over the salad, and give it a final toss before serving.

VEGETARIAN MAINS

SPANISH RICE

COOK TIME: 35 MIN | SERVES: 3

Ingredients:

- ½ cup asparagus, tough ends removed. Good parts washed and chopped
- 1 cup red bell peppers, sliced
- 8 oz white mushrooms, thinly sliced
- ½ cup canned green peppers, onions, and diced tomatoes, with their juices
- ½ cup canned garbanzo beans, drained and rinsed
- 3 tbsp chili sauce
- 2 tbsp lime juice
- 2 tbsp nutritional yeast
- 2 tbsp spice blend
- ½ sheet nori, crumbled up
- 1 cup uncooked red rice
- 2 cups boiling water
- Aluminum foil

Directions:

1. Preheat the air fryer to 400°F, or 200°C.

2. In a metal roasting pan that can fit in your air fryer, add together the chopped asparagus, sliced red bell peppers, sliced mushrooms, diced tomatoes, garbanzo beans, chili sauce, lime juice, nutritional yeast, spice blend, and crumbled nori. Mix to combine.

3. Place the roasting pan in the air fryer, and roast for 10 minutes.

4. Add the uncooked red rice and boiling water to the roasting pan, and mix. Carefully cover the pan tightly with aluminum foil, and roast for 22 minutes. Remove the aluminum foil, mix, and continue roasting for an extra 3 minutes, or until the top is crisped.

5. Allow the rice mixture to cool slightly. Stir once more, and serve warm.

Substitution tip: if you don't want to use crumbled nori, you can use 1 tsp dulse granules.

VEGETARIAN MAINS

STUFFED EGGPLANT

COOK TIME: 30 MIN | SERVES: 2

Ingredients:

- 2 medium eggplants
- 1 (16 oz) can kidney beans, drained and rinsed
- 2 spring onions, both white and green parts finely sliced
- 1 tbsp chili sauce
- 2 tsp mild taco seasoning
- 2 tbsp lemon juice
- ¼ cup lemon-tahini dressing

Directions:

1. Preheat the air fryer to 400°F, or 200°C.

2. Place the whole eggplants in the air fryer basket, and roast for 30 minutes.

3. In a medium-sized mixing bowl, add together the kidney beans, sliced spring onions, chili sauce, mild taco seasoning, and lemon juice. Mix to combine, and set aside.

4. Gently remove the eggplants from the air fryer, and cut each in half lengthwise.

5. Carefully fill each eggplant with half of the kidney bean mixture. Then drizzle half of the lemon-tahini dressing over each. Serve warm.

VEGETARIAN MAINS

GARBANZO BEAN TORTILLAS

COOK TIME: 10 MIN | MAKES: 8

Ingredients:

- 8 small flour tortillas
- 1½ cups vegan mozzarella cheese, shredded
- 1 cup canned garbanzo beans, drained and rinsed
- ½ cup parsley, finely chopped
- 10 oz mild Pico de Gallo salsa

Directions:

1. Preheat the air fryer to 380°F, or 193°C.

2. In a medium-sized mixing bowl, add together the shredded vegan cheese, garbanzo beans, and chopped parsley, and mix to combine.

3. Evenly divide the cheese mixture between the tortillas, placing a dollop in the middle of each one. Fold the tortillas in half.

4. Place 4 tortillas in the fryer basket, and cook for 4 to 5 minutes, until the cheese has melted, and the tops are golden and crispy.

5. Transfer the filled tortillas onto a platter, and serve immediately with the mild Pico de Gallo salsa.

Ingredient tip: add chopped avocado into the mozzarella and garbanzo bean mixture to add a creamy texture.

VEGETARIAN MAINS

CRUMBED TOMATOES

COOK TIME: 20 MIN | MAKES: 4

Ingredients:

- Nonstick cooking spray
- ¼ cup vegan mayonnaise
- 2 tbsp unsweetened almond milk
- 1 cup panko breadcrumbs
- ½ tsp cayenne pepper
- 2 large green tomatoes, thickly sliced

For serving:
- Vegan mayonnaise
- 4 vegan rolls
- Hamburger dill pickles
- Rocket

Directions:

1. Set the air fryer temperature to 400°F, or 200°C. Coat the air fryer basket with nonstick cooking spray.

2. In a small mixing bowl, add together the vegan mayonnaise and almond milk, and whisk to combine.

3. In a separate small bowl, combine the panko breadcrumbs and cayenne pepper.

4. Pat the tomato slices dry with paper towels, to remove excess liquid.

5. Dip the tomato slices in the mayonnaise mixture to coat both sides. Then place them into the breadcrumb mixture, and coat both sides.

6. Place half the coated tomato slices in the fryer basket.

7. Cook for 8 to 10 minutes, until the breadcrumbs are crispy and golden brown.

8. Transfer the crispy tomato slices onto a plate. Spread a thin layer of vegan mayonnaise on the rolls, and top with 2 crispy tomato slices, dill pickles, and rocket. Serve immediately.

VEGETARIAN MAINS

TOMATO ROTINI

COOK TIME: 18 MIN | SERVES: 3

Ingredients:

- Aluminum foil
- 1½ cups canned diced tomatoes with their juices
- 1 tbsp garlic, minced
- 1 tsp onion powder
- ¾ tsp dried thyme
- ¾ tsp dried oregano
- 2 tbsp lime juice
- ½ of a (16 oz) box uncooked rotini pasta
- 3 to 4 cups boiling water

Directions:

1. Preheat the air fryer to 400°F, or 200°C.

2. In a small metal roasting pan, add together the diced tomatoes with their juices, minced garlic, onion powder, dried thyme, dried oregano, and lime juice. Mix to combine, cover tightly with aluminum foil, and bake for 6 minutes.

3. Place the uncooked rotini in another metal roasting pan, and pour enough boiling water over the pasta to completely cover it. Cover the roasting pan tightly with aluminum foil.

4. Place the pasta pan in the air fryer, on top of the pan with the sauce. Bake for 9 minutes.

5. Remove both pans from the air fryer, and remove the foil. Drain the pasta in a colander, and return it to the pan. Pour the sauce over the rotini pasta, and mix to coat.

6. Re-cover the pan with the foil, and bake for 3 minutes, or until the pasta and sauce are heated through, and bubbling. Mix before serving.

VEGETARIAN MAINS

BLACK BEAN PATTIES

COOK TIME: 15 MIN | MAKES: 4

Ingredients:

For the onions:
- ¼ cup water
- 2 tbsp apple cider vinegar
- 1 tbsp granulated sugar
- 1 tsp fine salt
- ½ large red onion, thinly sliced

For the patties:
- 3 tsp olive oil, plus more
- ½ red onion, diced
- 2 tsp fine salt, divided
- 1 tsp ground black pepper
- 15 oz canned black beans, drained (not rinsed), liquid reserved
- ½ cup carrots, grated
- ½ cup cilantro, chopped
- ½ tbsp garlic, minced
- ¾ tsp ground coriander
- 1 tsp whole-grain mustard
- 1 tbsp tahini
- ¼ cup all-purpose flour

Directions:

For the onions:

1. Preheat the air fryer to 380°F, or 193°C.

2. In a small stockpot over medium heat, add together the water, apple cider vinegar, granulated sugar, and fine salt. Mix to combine, and allow to boil. Add the sliced red onion, and turn off the heat. Set aside.

For the patties:

1. In a medium-sized, heavy bottom pan over medium heat, add together the olive oil, diced red onion, 1 tsp fine salt, and 1 tsp ground black pepper. Mix to combine, and fry for 2 to 3 minutes until softened.

2. In a food processor, add together the fried red onion, black beans, grated carrots, chopped cilantro, minced garlic, ground coriander, whole-grain mustard, tahini, all-purpose flour, and the remaining 1 tsp salt. Pulse until just combined.

3. Form the mixture into 4 equally-sized patties, and brush them with olive oil.

4. Place the patties in the fryer basket, and cook for 15 minutes until golden brown.

5. Remove the patties from the air fryer basket, and serve with the pickled red onions.

Tip: you can serve these patties on vegan whole-grain buns, with rocket and sliced tomatoes.

VEGETARIAN MAINS

SHIITAKE QUINOA

COOK TIME: 37 MIN | SERVES: 4

Ingredients:

- Olive oil cooking spray
- 2 tbsp sunflower oil
- 8 oz shiitake mushrooms, diced
- ½ red onion, diced
- 1 tbsp garlic, minced
- 1 cup quinoa
- 2 cups vegetable stock
- 1 tbsp basil, chopped
- ½ tsp fine salt
- ¼ tsp cayenne pepper
- Fresh cilantro for garnish

Directions:

1. Preheat the air fryer to 380°F, or 193°C. Spray the inside of a 5-cup capacity casserole dish with olive oil cooking spray.

2. In a large frying pan, heat the sunflower oil over medium heat. Add the diced mushrooms and diced red onions, and cook for 5 minutes, stirring occasionally, until the mushrooms begin to brown.

3. Add the minced garlic, and cook for 2 minutes. Transfer the vegetables into a large mixing bowl. Add the quinoa, vegetable stock, chopped basil, fine salt, and cayenne pepper, and mix to combine.

4. Transfer the quinoa and vegetable mixture into the prepared casserole dish, and place the dish into the air fryer. Cook for 15 minutes.

5. Stir, and reduce the heat to 360°F, or 182°C. Then return the quinoa to the air fryer, and bake for an extra 15 minutes.

6. Remove from the air fryer, and allow to sit for 5 minutes, before fluffing with a fork, and topping with cilantro.

VEGETARIAN MAINS

MEDITERRANEAN EGGPLANT

COOK TIME: 25 MIN | SERVES: 4

Ingredients:

- 1 large egg
- 1 tbsp water
- ½ cup plain breadcrumbs
- 1 tsp garlic powder
- 1 tsp onion powder
- ½ tsp dried oregano
- ½ tsp fine salt
- ½ tsp smoked paprika
- 1 medium eggplant, sliced into thick rounds
- 2 tbsp olive oil
- 4 tsp olive paste

Directions:

1. Preheat the air fryer to 360°F, or 182°C.

2. In a medium-sized, shallow bowl, beat the egg and water together, until frothy.

3. In a separate medium-sized, shallow bowl, add together the plain breadcrumbs, garlic powder, onion powder, dried oregano, fine salt, and smoked paprika. Mix to combine.

4. Coat each eggplant slice in the egg mixture, then place it into the breadcrumb mixture, making sure it's evenly coated. Place the eggplant slices in a single layer at the bottom of the air fryer basket.

5. Drizzle the tops of the eggplant slices with the olive oil, then fry for 15 minutes. Flip each slice, and cook for an extra 10 minutes. Serve warm, with 1 tsp of olive paste on each eggplant slice.

VEGETARIAN MAINS

TOFU CURRY

COOK TIME: 25 MIN | SERVES: 2

Ingredients:

- 1 cup canned diced tomatoes with their juices
- 2 cups unsweetened plain soy milk
- 2 tbsp lemon juice
- 1 tbsp spice blend
- 2 tbsp mild curry powder
- 1 tsp ground ginger
- ½ tsp ground cumin
- 1 (12 oz) bag frozen broccoli, thawed
- ½ (16-ounce) block super firm tofu, cubed
- 2 tbsp fresh coriander, finely chopped

Directions:

1. Preheat the air fryer to 375°F, or 190°C.

2. In a large metal roasting pan, add together the diced tomatoes with their juices, soy milk, lemon juice, spice blend, mild curry powder, ground ginger, and ground cumin. Mix to combine. Add the thawed broccoli and super firm tofu cubes to the pan, and mix to coat.

3. Place the roasting pan in the air fryer, and roast for 15 minutes. Stir the curry, and continue to roast for another 10 minutes, or until the curry is bubbling.

4. Remove the roasting pan from the air fryer, and mix in the chopped coriander. Serve warm.

Substitution tip: you can replace soy milk with coconut milk or coconut cream.

VEGETARIAN MAINS

KALE PIZZA

COOK TIME: 32 MIN | MAKES: 4

Ingredients:

- ½ cup jarred roasted garlic tomato sauce
- 1 tsp dried basil
- 1 tsp garlic, crushed
- 1 lb. frozen pizza dough, thawed
- 1 cup kale, roughly chopped
- ½ cup vegan mozzarella, shredded

Directions:

1. Preheat the air fryer to 400°F, or 200°C.

2. In a small mixing bowl, add together the roasted garlic tomato sauce, fried basil, and crushed garlic. Mix to combine, and set aside.

3. Divide the pizza dough into 4 balls, and roll out each ball into a 6-inch round pizza crust.

4. Place one pizza crust in the air fryer basket. Spread 1 tbsp of the tomato sauce mixture over the crust.

5. Cover the sauce with one-quarter of the chopped kale, and top the pizza with shredded vegan mozzarella cheese, evenly spread.

6. Grill the pizza for 8 minutes, or until the crust is crispy. Repeat with the remaining pizzas, and serve warm.

VEGETARIAN MAINS

SAMBAL BRUSSELS SPROUTS

COOK TIME: 18 MIN | MAKES: 4 CUPS

Ingredients:

For the sauce:
- ½ tsp olive oil
- 2 tsp garlic, minced
- 1 tbsp honey
- 2 tsp granulated sugar
- 1 tbsp lime juice
- 1 tbsp apple cider vinegar
- 1 tbsp sambal oelek

For the Brussels sprouts:
- ½ lb. Brussels sprouts, stems removed, cut in half
- 3 tsp olive oil
- ½ tsp fine salt

Directions:

To make the sauce:

1. In a small stockpot over low heat, add together the olive oil, minced garlic, honey, granulated sugar, lime juice, apple cider vinegar, and sambal oelek. Mix to combine, and cook for 2 to 3 minutes, until slightly thickened.

2. Remove from the heat, cover, and set aside.

To make the Brussels sprouts:

1. Preheat the air fryer to 390°F, or 198°C.

2. Place the cut Brussels sprouts in a small mixing bowl, add the olive oil and fine salt, and toss to coat.

3. Place the coated Brussels sprouts into the basket, and fry for 15 minutes, stopping half way through to toss them.

4. Once the sprouts are crispy, and the centers are tender, transfer them into a medium-sized serving bowl.

5. Drizzle with the sauce, and toss to coat. Serve warm.

VEGETARIAN MAINS

BBQ BROCCOLI BITES

COOK TIME: 8 MIN | SERVES: 4

Ingredients:

- 3 large eggs, beaten
- ½ cup all-purpose flour
- 16 oz broccoli florets, cut into bite size pieces
- Olive oil cooking spray
- 5 tbsp barbecue sauce
- 2 tbsp unsalted butter, melted
- Store-bought blue cheese dip
- Carrot sticks, for serving

Directions:

1. Preheat the air fryer to 380°F, or 193°C.

2. Place the beaten eggs in a small mixing bowl, and place the all-purpose flour in a separate medium-sized bowl. Dip the broccoli florets into the beaten egg, then into the flour to coat. Shake off the excess. Place the florets coated on a work surface, and spray both sides with olive oil cooking spray.

3. Arrange a single layer of the coated broccoli in the air fryer basket. Cook for 7 to 8 minutes, until golden and tender. Repeat with the remaining broccoli.

4. Return all the broccoli to the air fryer, and cook for 1 minute to heat through. Transfer to a large bowl, and toss with the barbecue sauce and melted butter.

5. Serve with store-bought blue cheese dip, and carrot sticks.

SIDES

SIDES

MOZZARELLA POTATO BAKE

COOK TIME: 32 MIN | SERVES: 2

INGREDIENTS:

- 2 large russet potatoes, washed and dried
- Olive oil cooking spray
- 3 tbsp unsalted butter, cut into small pieces
- 1 tsp fine salt
- 1 tsp ground black pepper
- 1 tbsp parsley, finely chopped
- ½ cup part-skim mozzarella cheese, shredded

DIRECTIONS:

1. Preheat the air fryer to 350°F, or 176°C. Line the bottom of the air fryer basket with parchment liner.

2. Cut the potatoes crosswise, into thin slices, but make sure to leave enough at the bottom so that the potato stays joined together (Hasselback technique).

3. Transfer the potatoes into the air fryer basket, and spray with olive oil cooking spray. Bake for 15 minutes.

4. Remove the air fryer basket, and place the unsalted butter in between the potato slices. Sprinkle with fine salt, ground black pepper, and chopped parsley. Return the basket to the air fryer, and bake for another 15 minutes.

5. Remove the fryer basket, and stuff the potato slices with shredded mozzarella cheese.

6. Bake for another 1 to 2 minutes, or until the cheese has melted. Serve warm.

Tip: To ensure that you don't go all the way through when slicing the potato, lay the potato between 2 wooden spoons on the counter, and slice until the knife touches the wooden spoon handles, then stop.

FETA SWEET POTATO

COOK TIME: 22 MIN | SERVES: 2

Ingredients:

- 1 small red onion, minced
- 1 tsp lime zest, plus 2 tbsp juice
- 2 lb. sweet potatoes, peeled, and cut into pieces
- 4 tsp olive oil, divided
- 2 tsp ground thyme
- ½ tsp sea salt
- Olive oil cooking spray
- 2 oz feta cheese, cut into pieces
- 2 tsp honey
- ¼ tsp ground black pepper
- 2 cups rocket
- ¼ cup pumpkin seeds, toasted

Directions:

1. Preheat the air fryer to 400°F, or 200°C.

2. In small mixing bowl, combine the minced onion and lime juice. Mix, and set aside.

3. In a large mixing bowl, combine the sweet potato pieces, 1 tsp olive oil, ground thyme, and sea salt. Toss to coat. Place the sweet potatoes in even layer in the air fryer basket, and place it into the air fryer. Cook for 16 to 22 minutes, until the sweet potatoes are tender and browned.

4. Transfer the sweet potatoes to a large bowl, and set aside. Spray the bottom of the air fryer basket with olive oil cooking spray, scatter the feta pieces in the basket, and spray the feta with olive oil cooking spray. Return the basket to the fryer, and cook for 4 to 6 minutes, until the feta is lightly browned.

5. Add the honey, ground black pepper, lime zest, and remaining 1 tbsp olive oil into the red onion mixture, and mix to combine. Add the onion mixture to the sweet potatoes, and toss to coat.

6. Add the rocket and toasted pumpkin seeds, and toss to combine.

7. Season with sea salt and ground black pepper to taste. Transfer to a serving platter, top with feta cheese, and serve.

SIDES

ROMANO BROCCOLI DIP

COOK TIME: 25 MIN | SERVES: 8

- 1 cup broccoli florets, fresh or frozen
- ½ red onion, roughly chopped
- 2 tbsp sunflower oil
- ½ cup unsweetened soy milk
- 3 cups sweet peas, frozen
- 1½ tbsp garlic, minced
- 2 tbsp oregano, chopped
- 1 tsp rosemary, stems removed, chopped
- ½ tsp fine salt
- ½ tsp ground black pepper
- Shredded Romano cheese, for garnish
- Fresh cilantro, for garnish

DIRECTIONS:

1. Preheat the air fryer to 380°F, or 193°C.

2. In a large mixing bowl, combine the broccoli florets, chopped onion, and sunflower oil, and toss to coat.

3. Place the broccoli into the air fryer basket in an even layer, and bake for 15 minutes.

4. Place the broccoli in a food processor, add the soy milk, and pulse until smooth.

5. In a medium-sized stockpot, add together the broccoli puree, sweet peas, minced garlic, chopped oregano, chopped rosemary, fine salt, and ground black pepper. Mix to combine.

6. Cook over medium heat for 10 minutes, stirring regularly.

7. Serve with shredded Parmesan cheese and chopped cilantro.

MEXICAN STUFFED POBLANO

COOK TIME: 36 MIN | MAKES: 2

Ingredients:

For the chili sauce:
- 1 tbsp sunflower oil
- ¼ cup red onion, finely chopped
- ¼ cup tomato paste
- 1 tbsp chili powder
- 1 tsp garlic, crushed
- 1 tsp dried rosemary
- 1 tsp ground cumin
- ¼ tsp fine salt
- 1 cup chicken broth

For the peppers:
- 2 poblano peppers, rinsed and dried
- 1 cup part-skim mozzarella cheese, shredded
- ½ cup canned corn kernels
- 1 tbsp parsley, chopped
- ¼ tsp fine salt
- ¼ tsp ground black pepper
- 1 tbsp sour cream

Directions:

For the chili sauce:

1. In a small stockpot over medium heat, combine the sunflower oil and chopped onion, and cook for 5 minutes until the onion is translucent.

2. Add the tomato paste, chili powder, crushed garlic, dried rosemary, ground cumin, and fine salt, and cook for 1 minute, stirring occasionally.

3. Pour in the chicken broth, and allow the mixture to simmer for 5 minutes. Remove from the heat, cover, and set aside.

For the peppers:

1. Preheat the air fryer to 400°F, or 200°C.

2. Place the poblano peppers in the air fryer basket, and roast for 10 minutes, flipping them half way, until the skin is slightly charred.

3. Remove the peppers from the air fryer, place them in an airtight container, and allow them to steam for 5

minutes.

4. Once the peppers are cool enough to handle, peel the skins off, and discard.

5. In a medium-sized mixing bowl, add together the shredded mozzarella cheese, corn kernels, chopped parsley, fine salt, and ground black pepper. Mix to combine.

6. Make a slit down the middle of each of the roasted peppers, from the stem to the tip, keeping the peppers intact. Remove the seeds.

7. Divide the cheese and corn mixture in half, and stuff half into each pepper.

8. Transfer the stuffed peppers into a shallow roasting pan that can fit your air fryer.

9. Place the pan in the air fryer basket, and roast for 10 minutes, until the cheese has melted.

10. Spoon the red chili sauce over the peppers, and top with the sour cream when serving.

SIDES

GREEK RICE BALLS

COOK TIME: 11 MIN | SERVES: 6

Ingredients:

- ½ cup cooked green lentils
- 1 tbsp garlic, minced
- ¼ yellow onion, minced
- ¼ cup cilantro leaves
- 6 basil leaves
- 1 cup long grain rice, cooked
- 1 tbsp lime juice
- 1 tbsp olive oil
- ½ tsp fine salt

Directions:

1. Preheat the air fryer to 380°F, or 193°C.

2. In a food processor, combine the cooked lentils, minced garlic, minced onion, cilantro, and basil, and pulse until mostly smooth.

3. Transfer the lentil mixture into a large mixing bowl, and add the cooked long grain rice, lime juice, olive oil, and fine salt. Mix to combine.

4. Mold the rice mixture into 6 balls, and place them in a single layer in the air fryer basket, spaced evenly apart.

5. Fry for 6 minutes. Turn the rice balls, and then fry for an extra 4 to 5 minutes, until browned on all sides.

LEMON & LIME FENNEL

COOK TIME: 20 MIN | SERVES: 2

INGREDIENTS:

- 1 fennel bulb, base lightly trimmed
- 2 tbsp olive oil, divided
- 1 tbsp water
- ¼ tsp sea salt
- ¼ tsp ground black pepper
- 2 tbsp dill, roughly chopped
- 2 tsp honey
- 1½ tsp apple cider vinegar
- ⅛ tsp grated lemon zest, plus 1 tbsp lemon juice
- ⅛ tsp grated lime zest, plus 1 tbsp lime juice

DIRECTIONS:

1. Preheat the air fryer to 350°F, or 176°C.

2. Cut the fennel bulb lengthwise to make 8 wedges (do not remove the core). In a large mixing bowl, combine 1 tbsp olive oil, the water, sea salt, and ground black pepper. Whisk until the salt has dissolved. Add the fennel wedges, and toss to coat.

3. Place the fennel wedges in the air fryer basket. Place the basket into the air fryer, and cook for 12 to 20 minutes, flipping half way, until tender and browned.

4. In a small mixing bowl, add together the chopped dill, honey, apple cider vinegar, lemon zest and lemon juice, lime zest and lime juice, and the remaining 1 tbsp olive oil. Whisk to combine, and season with sea salt and ground black pepper to taste.

5. Transfer the fennel wedges onto a serving platter, and drizzle with the lemon and lime dressing. Serve warm.

ZUCCHINI FRIES

COOK TIME: 12 MIN | SERVES: 2-4

Ingredients:

- 1 large zucchini, quartered lengthwise
- ¾ cup panko breadcrumbs
- 2 tbsp sunflower oil
- ½ cup Romano cheese, grated
- 1 large egg
- 1 tablespoon all-purpose flour
- ½ tsp dried oregano
- Fine salt
- Ground black pepper
- Olive oil cooking spray
- ½ cup plain Greek yogurt
- ½ tsp grated lime zest, plus 1 tbsp juice

Directions:

1. Preheat the air fryer to 400°F, or 200°C.

2. Use a vegetable peeler to shave the seeds from the inner portion of each zucchini quarter. Halve each quarter lengthwise, then cut in half crosswise, to make 16 pieces.

3. In a medium-sized, microwave-safe bowl, combine the breadcrumbs and sunflower oil, and toss to coat. Microwave for 1 to 3 minutes, stirring frequently, until golden brown.

4. Transfer to a shallow dish, allow to cool slightly, then mix in the grated Romano cheese. In a separate shallow dish, add together the egg, all-purpose flour, dried oregano, ¼ tsp fine salt, and ⅛ tsp ground black pepper. Mix to combine.

5. Working with a few zucchini pieces at a time, coat them in the egg mixture, letting the excess drip off. Then coat them in the breadcrumb mixture, and transfer to a large plate.

6. Lightly spray the air fryer basket with olive oil cooking spray. Place half of the zucchini pieces in the prepared basket, spaced evenly apart. Arrange the remaining zucchini pieces on top, perpendicular to the first layer. Place the basket in the air fryer, and cook for 10 to 12 minutes, until the zucchini is tender and crisp.

7. In a small mixing bowl, add together the Greek yogurt, lime zest and juice, ¼ tsp fine salt, and ⅛ tsp ground black pepper. Whisk to combine.

8. Transfer the zucchini fries onto a serving platter, and season with fine salt and ground black pepper to taste. Serve with lime yogurt sauce.

SIDES

GARBANZO TURKEY SALAD

COOK TIME: 15 MIN | SERVES: 2

Ingredients:

- 2 tbsp olive oil
- ½ tbsp garlic, minced
- 2 tsp smoked paprika
- ⅛ tsp sea salt
- 12 oz boneless, skinless turkey breasts, cut into pieces
- 1 (15 oz) can garbanzo beans, rinsed
- 2 tbsp lime juice
- 2 large carrots, peeled and shredded
- 1 large cucumber, thinly sliced
- 2 tbsp mint, chopped
- 2 tbsp cilantro, chopped
- 2 tbsp dill, chopped
- ¼ cup feta cheese, cut into pieces
- ¼ cup pine nuts

Directions:

1. Preheat the air fryer to 400°F, or 200°C.

2. In a large, microwave-safe bowl, add together the olive oil, minced garlic, smoked paprika, and sea salt. Mix to combine, and microwave for 1 minute, stirring half way through, until fragrant.

3. Place the turkey pieces, garbanzo beans, and 2 tsp of the paprika oil mixture into the air fryer basket in an even layer. Place the basket into the air fryer, and cook for 10 to 15 minutes, stirring half way, until the turkey pieces are fully cooked.

4. Add the turkey pieces, garbanzo beans, lime juice, shredded carrots, sliced cucumber, chopped mint, chopped cilantro, chopped dill, feta pieces, and pine nuts into the remaining paprika oil mixture, and toss to combine. Season with sea salt and ground black pepper to taste, and serve immediately.

Substitution tip: you can use chicken, beef, or tinned tuna in this recipe.

SIDES

ORANGE ZUCCHINIS

COOK TIME: 10 MIN | SERVES: 4

Ingredients:

- ¼ cup orange juice
- 1 tbsp grated orange zest
- 1 tbsp honey
- 1 tbsp balsamic vinegar
- 2 large zucchinis, cut into chunks

Directions:

1. Preheat the air fryer to 400°F, or 200°C.

2. In a large mixing bowl, add together the orange juice, orange zest, honey, and balsamic vinegar. Mix to combine. Add the zucchini chunks, and toss to coat.

3. Transfer the seasoned zucchinis to the air fryer basket, and roast for 10 minutes, until fully cooked.

Substitution tip: you can use any type of vegetables for this recipe; Brussels sprouts, sweet potato, green beans, or russet potatoes.

SIDES

HERB EGGPLANT SALAD

COOK TIME: 12 MIN | SERVES: 2

Ingredients:

- 2 eggplants, cut into chunks
- 2 tbsp sunflower oil, divided
- ¼ tsp sea salt, divided
- ⅛ tsp ground black pepper
- 1 red onion, thinly sliced
- 2 tsp lime juice
- 2 tsp thyme, minced
- 2 tsp rosemary, minced
- 2 tsp oregano, minced
- 2 tsp marjoram, minced
- 2 tsp sage, minced

Directions:

1. Preheat the air fryer to 400°F, or 200°C.

2. In large mixing bowl, combine the eggplant chunks, 1 tbsp sunflower oil, ⅛ tsp sea salt, and ground black pepper. Toss to coat.

3. Spread the eggplant mixture evenly in the air fryer basket. Place the basket into the air fryer, and cook for 8 to 12 minutes, until the eggplant has softened.

4. Add the sliced onion into the eggplant mixture, and mix. Return the basket to the air fryer, and cook for 2 to 4 minutes, until the eggplant has browned.

5. In the now-empty bowl, add together the lime juice, minced thyme, minced rosemary, minced oregano, minced marjoram, minced sage, remaining 1 tbsp sunflower oil, and remaining ⅛ tsp sea salt. Mix to combine. Add the cooked eggplant into the herb mixture, and toss to coat. Season with sea salt and ground black pepper to taste, and serve.

SIDES

TORTILLA CRISPS

COOK TIME: 10 MIN | SERVES: 2

INGREDIENTS:

- 2 flour tortillas
- Olive oil cooking spray
- ⅛ tsp fine salt
- ⅛ tsp ground black pepper

DIRECTIONS:

1. Preheat the air fryer to 300°F, or 148°C.

2. Cut the tortillas into eight triangles, and lightly spray both sides of each triangle with olive oil cooking spray. Sprinkle with fine salt and ground black pepper.

3. Place the tortilla triangles in an even layer in the air fryer basket. Place the basket into the air fryer, and cook for 3 to 5 minutes, until the triangles are golden brown on the edges.

4. Use tongs to gently flip and redistribute the triangles, and continue to cook for 3 to 5 minutes, until golden brown, and crisp.

5. Allow to cool completely before serving.

Tip: you can eat the tortilla crisps as is, or serve with hummus or guacamole.

BALSAMIC GREEN PEPPER

COOK TIME: 25 MIN | SERVES: 2

Ingredients:

- Plastic wrap
- 4 small green bell peppers, trimmed ½ inch from the top and bottom, seeds removed
- 2 tbsp sunflower oil
- 2 tbsp balsamic vinegar
- ½ tbsp garlic, minced
- Fine salt
- Ground black pepper
- 2 oz fresh mozzarella cheese, torn into pieces
- 2 tbsp basil, roughly chopped
- 1 tbsp sliced almonds

Directions:

1. Preheat the air fryer to 400°F, or 200°C.

2. Place the green bell peppers in the air fryer basket on their sides. Place the basket in the air fryer, and cook for 25 minutes, flipping and rotating them half way through cooking, until browned. Transfer the green peppers to a large bowl, cover tightly with plastic wrap, and allow them to steam for 10 minutes.

3. In a large serving bowl, add together the sunflower oil, balsamic vinegar, minced garlic, ⅛ tsp fine salt, and ⅛ tsp ground black pepper. Mix to combine.

4. Uncover the bowl, and let the peppers cool slightly. Once cool enough to handle, peel the bell peppers, and discard the skins. Then cut the bell peppers into strips, and add the strips and fresh mozzarella into the bowl with the balsamic dressing. Toss to coat, and season with fine salt and ground black pepper to taste. Sprinkle with chopped basil and sliced almonds, and serve.

SIDES

CHILI & LIME CORN

COOK TIME: 7 MIN | SERVES: 4

Ingredients:

- 4 medium ears of corn on the cob
- Olive oil cooking spray
- 2 tbsp lite mayonnaise
- 1 tbsp lime juice
- 1 tbsp grated lime zest
- ½ tsp chili powder
- ¼ tsp fine salt
- 2 oz feta cheese, crumbled
- 1 tbsp parsley, finely chopped

Directions:

1. Preheat the air fryer to 375°F, or 190°C.

2. Spray the corn with olive oil cooking spray. Working in batches, place the corn cobs in the air fryer basket in a single layer. Cook for 7 minutes, flipping half way, until the kernels are tender. Once the corn is cool enough to handle, cut the kernels off the cobs.

3. In a large mixing bowl, add together the lite mayonnaise, lime juice, lime zest, chili powder, and fine salt. Mix to combine.

4. Add the corn kernels, and mix. Transfer the coated corn onto a serving dish, and top with crumbled feta cheese, and chopped parsley. Serve immediately.

Tip: you can use frozen corn instead of using corn on the cob.

Substitution tip: you can replace the corn with sweet peas, garbanzo beans, or beans.

SIDES

SAVORY DINNER ROLLS

COOK TIME: 20 MIN | MAKES: 4

Ingredients:

- Parchment paper
- 1 cup plus 3 tbsp self-rising flour
- 1 tbsp granulated sugar
- ¼ cup unsalted butter, cut into pieces
- 1/3 cup shredded sharp cheddar cheese
- 2 tbsp bacon bits
- ½ cup plus 2 tbsp buttermilk
- ½ cup all-purpose flour, for dredging
- 2 tsp olive oil
- Fine salt
- Ground black pepper

Directions:

1. Preheat the air fryer to 380°F, or 193°C, leaving the basket inside.

2. Line a metal cake pan that can fit into your air fryer with parchment paper. Set aside.

3. In a large mixing bowl, add together the self-rising flour, granulated sugar, butter pieces, shredded cheddar cheese, and bacon bits. Mix to combine.

4. Add the buttermilk, and mix until well incorporated. The dough will be wet and sticky.

5. Place the all-purpose flour in a small bowl.

6. Divide the dough into 4 equal balls. Roll each ball of dough around in the flour, to coat evenly. Shake off the excess flour.

7. Transfer the flour-covered dough balls into the prepared cake pan, making sure they are all touching.

8. Place the pan in the air fryer basket, and bake for 20 minutes, keeping an eye on the rolls, until they are golden brown, and a toothpick inserted into the center comes out clean.

9. Brush the tops of the rolls with olive oil, sprinkle with fine salt and ground black pepper, and serve.

Tip: if the rolls are browning too fast, tent with aluminum foil.

SIDES

CRUMBED AVO

COOK TIME: 12 MIN | SERVES: 2

Ingredients:

- Nonstick cooking spray
- 2 ripe avocados, halved and pitted
- ½ cup aquafaba (canned garbanzo bean liquid)
- 1½ cups plain breadcrumbs
- ½ tsp fine salt
- ½ tsp ground black pepper

Directions:

1. Preheat the air fryer to 390°F, or 198°C.

2. Spray the fryer basket with nonstick cooking spray.

3. Slice the avocado into 8 wedges. Place the aquafaba and plain breadcrumbs in separate medium-sized bowls. Dip the avocado wedges in the aquafaba, and then in the plain breadcrumbs.

4. Place the wedges in the fryer basket, and cook for 5 to 6 minutes, until golden.

5. Transfer the crumbed avocado wedges onto a platter, and sprinkle the fine salt and ground black pepper on top. Serve immediately.

SIDES

CORIANDER PARSNIPS

COOK TIME: 30 MIN | SERVES: 4

Ingredients:

- 2 tbsp unsalted butter
- 1 tbsp maple syrup
- ½ tsp grated lemon zest, plus 1 tbsp juice
- ½ tsp ground coriander
- Fine salt
- Ground black pepper
- 2 lb. parsnips, peeled, and cut into quarters lengthwise
- 1 tbsp spring onions, chopped

Directions:

1. Preheat the air fryer to 400°F, or 200°C.

2. In large, microwave-safe mixing bowl, combine the butter, maple syrup, lemon zest, ground coriander, and ¼ tsp fine salt. Microwave for 1 minute, stirring occasionally, until the butter is melted. Whisk to combine. In small mixing bowl, combine 1 tbsp of the butter mixture, and the lemon juice, and set aside. Add the cut parsnips to the remaining butter mixture, and toss to coat. Place into the air fryer basket.

3. Place the basket into the air fryer, and cook for 30 minutes, tossing occasionally, until tender and browned.

4. Transfer the parsnips back into their now-empty bowl, and toss with the reserved butter mixture. Season with fine salt and ground black pepper to taste, and sprinkle with chopped spring onions before serving.

DESSERTS

DESSERTS

STRAWBERRY PIE

COOK TIME: 15 MIN | SERVES: 4

INGREDIENTS:

- Non-stick cooking spray
- ¼ cup granulated sugar
- 2 tbsp cornstarch
- ¼ tsp vanilla extract
- ½ tsp grated lemon zest
- 2½ cups strawberries, sliced
- 1 store-bought piecrust
- 1 large egg

DIRECTIONS:

1. Preheat the air fryer to 350°F, or 176°C.

2. Spray a mini pie dish with nonstick cooking spray.

3. In a medium-sized mixing bowl, add together the granulated sugar, cornstarch, vanilla extract, and lemon zest, and mix to combine. Add the strawberry slices, and toss to coat. Transfer the mixture to the pie dish.

4. Lay the dough on a work surface, then cut out a round shape that will cover your pie dish. Place the dough over the baking dish and filling, and crimp the edges to create a seal. Cut 4 slits around the center of the dough.

5. In a small mixing bowl, beat the large egg with 1 tbsp water. Use a pastry brush to coat the dough with the egg wash.

6. Place the pie in the air fryer basket. Bake for 15 minutes, until the crust is golden, and the pie is bubbling. Allow the pie to cool for 15 minutes before cutting. Serve warm, with fresh whipped cream or ice cream.

Tip: use all the dough by making a crust for the bottom of the pie.

DESSERTS

PEACHES & CREAM

COOK TIME: 10 MIN | SERVES: 4

INGREDIENTS:

- 5 peaches, halved and pitted
- 1 cup vanilla bean ice cream
- 2 tbsp pecan nuts, chopped
- Honey, for garnish

DIRECTIONS:

1. Preheat the air fryer to 375°F, or 190°C.

2. Place a single layer of the halved peaches, cut sides up, in the air fryer basket. Cook for 10 minutes, until the peaches are soft and golden brown.

3. Place the peaches in 4 serving bowls. Add 2 heaped tbsp of vanilla bean ice cream into the center of each peach half. Top with chopped pecan nuts, and drizzle over the honey. Serve immediately.

DESSERTS

CINNAMON CAKE BITES

COOK TIME: 10 MIN | MAKES: 3 CUPS

Ingredients:

For the sauce:
- ¼ cup cream cheese, at room temperature
- 3 tbsp confectioner's sugar
- 1 tsp ground cinnamon
- 2 tsp unsalted butter, at room temperature
- 2 tsp whole milk

For the cake bites:
- ½ store-bought vanilla crème cake, cut into cubes
- 1 tbsp ground cinnamon
- ¼ cup granulated sugar
- Olive oil cooking spray

Directions:

For the sauce:
1. In a small mixing bowl, add together the cream cheese, confectioners' sugar, ground cinnamon, unsalted butter, and whole milk. Whisk to combine, and set aside.

For the cake bites:
1. Preheat the air fryer to 350°F, or 176°C.

2. In a large mixing bowl, combine the ground cinnamon and granulated sugar, and set aside.

3. Place the vanilla cake cubes in the air fryer basket, and coat with olive oil cooking spray.

4. Fry for 5 minutes, until golden brown.

5. Remove the cake bites from the fryer basket, and toss them in the cinnamon and sugar mixture, until well coat.

6. Repeat with any remaining cake bites, if needed.

7. Serve with the cinnamon cream cheese dipping sauce on the side.

Substitution tip: you can use any flavor of cake for this recipe.

DESSERTS

DATE CHOCO COOKIES

COOK TIME: 8 MIN | MAKES: 15

Ingredients:

- Parchment paper
- 1 tbsp ground flaxseeds
- 3 tbsp water
- 1 tsp vanilla extract
- 1 tsp apple cider vinegar
- 1/3 cup cashew butter
- ¼ cup date spread
- ¼ cup unsweetened cacao powder
- ¼ tsp baking soda
- ¼ cup dark chocolate chips

Directions:

1. Preheat the air fryer to 320°F, or 160°C, and line the air fryer basket with parchment paper.

2. In a medium-sized mixing bowl, add together the ground flaxseeds, water, vanilla extract, and apple cider vinegar. Whisk until well combined, and allow to sit for 5 minutes.

3. Add the cashew butter and date spread into the bowl with the mixture, and whisk to combine. Add the unsweetened cacao powder and baking soda, and whisk again.

4. Divide the dough into 2 tbsp balls, and top with a few dark chocolate chips. Place them in the air fryer, leaving some space for spreading.

5. Bake for 8 minutes, until the edges of the cookies start to go dark.

6. Allow the cookies to cool completely before taking them off the parchment paper. They will firm up and get crispy as they cool.

DESSERTS

SWEET POTATO WRAPS

COOK TIME: 10 MIN | MAKES: 4

INGREDIENTS:

- 1 can sweet potato puree
- ½ tsp ground cinnamon
- ½ tsp ground nutmeg
- ½ tsp ground allspice
- 4 egg roll wrappers
- Water, for brushing
- 2 tbsp unsalted butter, melted

DIRECTIONS:

1. Preheat the air fryer to 390°F, or 198°C.

2. In a medium-sized mixing bowl, combine the sweet potato puree, ground cinnamon, ground nutmeg and ground allspice. Mix until well incorporated.

3. Lay one egg roll wrapper in front of you, with a point facing towards you.

4. Spoon 2 to 3 tbsp of the sweet potato filling into the center of the wrapper, and use your hands to form it into a log shape, that runs lengthwise along the edge of the wrapper.

5. Fold the point of the wrapper nearest you over the filling, and pull gently to compact it even more.

6. Fold the sides in, and roll the wrapper away from you until you have some space left.

7. Dip a pastry brush in water, and run it along the edge of the wrapper. Then roll the wrapper up, smoothing the seam with your finger to help hold it in place.

8. Repeat with the remaining wrappers.

9. Place the roll-ups in the fryer basket, and brush with melted butter.

10. Bake for 10 minutes, turning them half way, until golden and crispy. Serve warm.

Substitution tip: in place of the sweet potato puree, place 3 to 4 blocks of chocolate in a row, and follow the same rolling method.

DESSERTS

CARAMEL APPLES

COOK TIME: 10 MIN | MAKES: 12

Ingredients:

- Parchment paper
- 2 granny smith apples, peeled and cored
- 1 large egg
- 1 tsp ground cinnamon
- ½ cup graham cracker crumbs
- ¼ cup all-purpose flour
- ⅛ tsp fine salt
- Olive oil cooking spray
- ¼ cup store-bought caramel topping

Directions:

1. Preheat the air fryer to 400°F, or 200°C, and line the air fryer basket with parchment paper.

2. Cut each granny smith apple into 6 wedges – you should have a total of 12 wedges.

3. In a small mixing bowl, beat the large egg and ground cinnamon until combined.

4. In a medium-sized mixing bowl, add together the graham cracker crumbs, all-purpose flour, and fine salt, and mix to combine.

5. Coat each apple wedge in the egg mixture, and then in the graham cracker crumb mixture.

6. Place the coated apples on the liner in the air fryer basket, and spray with olive oil cooking spray.

7. Fry for 4 to 5 minutes.

8. Flip the apples, and fry for an extra 4 to 5 minutes, until crisp.

9. Serve in bowls, and drizzle with the caramel topping.

Tip: if the caramel topping is too stiff, place it in a microwave-safe bowl, and microwave for 30 seconds, or until easy to pour.

DESSERTS

CARAMEL BANANA PASTRY

COOK TIME: 6 MIN | MAKES: 4

Ingredients:

- Parchment paper
- 1 can crescent rolls dough
- ¼ cup store-bought caramel topping
- 1 large banana

Directions:

1. Preheat the air fryer to 320°F, or 160°C, and line the air fryer basket with parchment paper.

2. Lay out 4 pieces of crescent dough on a flat surface.

3. Spread the caramel topping over the dough in a semi-thick layer.

4. Slice the banana in half widthwise, and then in half lengthwise, so you have 4 pieces. Place the banana pieces on top of the caramel topping.

5. Roll up the crescent dough, starting with the large end, and place them on the liner in the fryer basket.

6. Bake for 4 minutes.

7. Remove, turn the crescents over, and bake for another 2 minutes, or until golden brown. Serve warm.

DESSERTS

CHOCOLATE SLICES

COOK TIME: 20 MIN | MAKES: 4

Ingredients:

- Non-stick cooking spray
- ¼ cup cooked sweet potato, pureed
- ¼ cup date paste
- ¼ cup honey or maple syrup
- 2 tbsp ground flaxseeds
- 1 tbsp vanilla extract
- 1 tbsp water
- ¼ cup tapioca flour
- ¼ cup almond flour
- ½ tsp baking powder
- 2 tbsp unsweetened cocoa powder

Directions:

1. Preheat the air fryer to 320°F, or 160°C. Coat a round cake pan that can fit in your air fryer with non-stick cooking spray.

2. In a medium-sized mixing bowl, add together the sweet potato puree, date paste, honey or maple syrup, ground flaxseeds, vanilla extract, and water. Whisk to combine. Add the tapioca flour, almond flour, baking powder, and cocoa powder, and whisk to combine.

3. Transfer the batter into the cake pan. Wet your spatula, and smooth out the top of the batter.

4. Bake at for 20 minutes, or until a toothpick inserted into the middle comes out clean.

5. Allow the cake to cool before cutting into 4 slices.

DESSERTS

BERRY GANACHE CAKE

COOK TIME: 25 MIN | SERVES: 6

INGREDIENTS:

- Non-stick cooking spray
- 2 tbsp ground flaxseeds
- ½ cup milk, plus 1 tbsp
- 2 tbsp plain yogurt
- ¼ cup honey
- 1 tbsp apple cider vinegar
- 1 tbsp vanilla extract
- ¾ cup all-purpose flour
- 1 tsp baking powder
- ½ tsp baking soda
- ¼ cup dark chocolate chips
- 1/3 cup strawberry fruit spread

DIRECTIONS:

1. Preheat the air fryer to 350°F, or 176°C. Spray a round cake pan with non-stick cooking spray.

2. In a medium-sized mixing bowl, add together the ground flaxseeds, ½ cup milk, plain yogurt, honey, apple cider vinegar, and vanilla extract. Mix to combine, and then add the all-purpose flour, baking powder, and baking soda. Mix again.

3. Pour the batter evenly into the cake pan. Bake for 22 minutes, or until a toothpick inserted into the middle comes out clean. Allow the cake to cool completely in the pan.

4. Place the cake on a plate, and use a sharp knife to cut it in half horizontally, so that you have 2 equal layers. Set aside.

5. Turn the air fryer down to 300°F, or 148°C.

6. Place the dark chocolate chips in a small, heat-safe bowl in the air fryer for 3 minutes, or until the chocolate chips have melted.

7. Spread the strawberry fruit spread evenly over the top of the bottom layer of cake. Then place the top layer of cake over the fruit spread.

8. Remove the chocolate chips from the air fryer, and mix in the remaining 1 tbsp milk.

9. Spread the chocolate ganache quickly over the top layer of the cake, before the chocolate becomes too hard to spread. Cut the cake into 6 slices, and serve.

Tip: if your melted chocolate seizes, use ¼ tsp of olive oil at a time, until it smooths out.

DESSERTS

CITRUS SLICES

COOK TIME: 22 MIN | MAKES: 6

Ingredients:

- 4 tbsp coconut oil, melted
- ¼ tsp plus 1 pinch fine salt
- 1 tsp vanilla extract
- ½ cup plus 3 tbsp granulated sugar
- ½ cup plus 2 tbsp all-purpose flour
- ¼ cup orange juice
- 1 orange, zested
- ½ cup canned coconut cream
- 4 tbsp cornstarch
- Confectioner's sugar

Directions:

1. Set the air fryer temp to 350°F, or 176°C.

2. In a medium-sized mixing bowl, add together the coconut oil, ¼ tsp fine salt, vanilla extract, and 3 tbsp of granulated sugar. Mix to combine. Add the flour, and mix until a soft dough forms. Transfer the mixture to a baking dish, and gently press the dough to cover the bottom.

3. Place the dish in the fryer basket, and bake for 10 minutes until golden. Remove the crust from the fryer basket, and set aside to cool.

4. Heat a medium-sized stockpot over medium heat, and add the orange juice and orange zest, coconut cream, pinch of fine salt, and the remaining ½ cup of sugar. Whisk to combine. Whisk in the cornstarch, and cook for 5 minutes until thickened. Pour the orange mixture over the crust.

5. Place the dish in the fryer basket, and cook for 10 to 12 minutes, until the mixture is bubbling, and almost set.

6. Remove the dish from the fryer basket, and set aside to cool. Transfer the dish to the refrigerator for 4 hours. Dust with the confectioner's sugar, and slice into 6 bars before serving.

DESSERTS

CARROT CUPCAKES

COOK TIME: 15 MIN | MAKES: 6

Ingredients:

- 1 cup grated carrot
- 1/3 cup crushed pineapple
- ¼ cup golden raisins
- 2 tbsp honey
- 1/3 cup whole milk
- 1 cup almond flour
- 1 tsp ground cinnamon
- ½ tsp ground allspice
- 1 tsp baking powder
- ½ tsp baking soda
- 1/3 cup pecan nuts, chopped
- ½ cup store-bought cream cheese frosting

Directions:

1. Preheat the air fryer to 350°F, or 176°C. Make sure you have cupcake molds that will fit in your air fryer.

2. In a medium-sized mixing bowl, add together the grated carrot, crushed pineapple, golden raisins, honey, and whole milk. Mix to combine. Add the almond flour, ground cinnamon, allspice, baking powder, and baking soda, and mix until fully incorporated.

3. Divide the cake batter evenly between 6 cupcake molds. Sprinkle the chopped pecan nuts over each cupcake. Lightly press the walnuts into the batter so they are partially submerged.

4. Bake for 15 minutes, or until lightly browned, and a toothpick inserted into the middle comes out clean. Allow the muffins to cool completely, then spread on the cream cheese frosting before serving.

DESSERTS

BLUEBERRY SHORTCAKE

COOK TIME: 12 MIN | MAKES: 4 SLICES

Ingredients:

For the cream:
- 14oz canned coconut milk, refrigerated overnight
- 1½ tbsp confectioner's sugar
- 2 tsp lemon zest

For the shortcake:
- Non-stick cooking spray
- 1 cup all-purpose flour
- 2 tbsp granulated sugar
- 1½ tsp baking powder
- ⅛ tsp fine salt
- 2 tbsp sunflower oil
- ¼ cup unsweetened almond milk
- 2 cups fresh blueberries

Directions:

To make the cream:

1. Turn over the can of coconut milk, and open the bottom. Drain the liquid, and scoop the solids into the bowl of a stand mixer fitted with a whisk attachment.

2. Add the confectioner's sugar and lemon zest, and whisk for 2 to 3 minutes, until fluffy. Set aside.

For the shortcake:

1. Preheat the air fryer to 320°F, or 160°C. Coat a square baking dish that can fit your air fryer with non-stick cooking spray.

2. In a large mixing bowl, add together the all-purpose flour, granulated sugar, baking powder, and fine salt. Mix to combine. Add the sunflower oil, and use your fingertips to work the oil into the flour mixture, until it resembles fine breadcrumbs.

3. Add the almond milk, and use clean hands to mix. Don't overmix. Press the dough into the prepared baking dish.

4. Place the dish in the fryer basket, and bake for 12 minutes until the edges are golden.

5. Remove the dish from the fryer basket, and allow the shortcake to cool for 10 minutes.

6. Place the shortcake onto a serving platter, and cut it into 4 slices. Top each slice with 2 tbsp of coconut cream and ½ cup blueberries, before serving.

Tip: drizzle honey or maple syrup over the shortcake for extra flavor and sweetness.

DESSERTS

MOLTEN CHOCOLATE CAKE

COOK TIME: 10 MIN | SERVES: 4

Ingredients:

- Olive oil cooking spray
- ¼ cup all-purpose flour
- 1 tbsp unsweetened cocoa powder
- ⅛ tsp fine salt
- ½ tsp baking powder
- ¼ cup honey
- 1 large egg
- 2 tsp sunflower oil

Directions:

1. Preheat the air fryer to 380°F, or 193°C. Spray the insides of four ramekins with olive oil cooking spray.

2. In a medium-sized mixing bowl, add together the flour, cocoa powder, fine salt, baking powder, honey, large egg, and sunflower oil. Mix to combine.

3. Divide the batter evenly into the prepared ramekins.

4. Place the ramekins inside the air fryer, and bake for 10 minutes.

5. Remove the chocolate cakes from the air fryer, and slide a knife around the edge of each cake. Turn each ramekin upside down on a saucer, and serve. Dust with confectioner's sugar, if desired.

DESSERTS

PECAN & PEAR BAKE

COOK TIME: 20 MIN | MAKES: 2

Ingredients:

- 2 medium pears
- ¼ cup pecan nuts, chopped
- ¼ cup golden raisins
- 2 tbsp light brown sugar
- 3 tsp unsalted butter, melted
- ½ tsp ground cinnamon
- ½ tsp ground nutmeg
- ½ cup water

Directions:

1. Preheat the air fryer to 350°F, or 176°C.

2. Cut the tips off the pears so that they can stand. Remove the cores and some of the flesh, and discard.

3. Place the pears in a small baking pan that can fit your air fryer.

4. In a small mixing bowl, add together the chopped pecan nuts, golden raisins, light brown sugar, unsalted butter, ground cinnamon, and ground nutmeg. Mix to combine.

5. Spoon the sugar mixture into the centers of the hollowed-out pears.

6. Pour the water into the bottom of the air fryer pan.

7. Bake for 20 minutes, or until the pears are bubbling and fork-tender. Serve with fresh whipping cream or ice cream.

APPLE PIES

COOK TIME: 10 MIN | SERVES: 6

INGREDIENTS:

- 1 (9 oz) frozen puff pastry dough, thawed
- 6 tsp apple butter or apple preserves
- 2 honey crisp apples, cored, sliced, and divided
- 1 large egg, beaten

DIRECTIONS:

1. Preheat the air fryer to 350°F, or 176°C.

2. Cut the thawed puff pastry into 6 rectangles, and use a rolling pin to roll each piece out into a square.

3. Place a square of pastry on a work surface like a diamond. Spoon 1 tsp of the apple butter or apple preserves onto the bottom half, and spread it evenly at the bottom only. Top the apple preserves with some of the apple slices. Brush the edges of the pastry with some of the beaten egg, and fold the top corner over to form a triangle.

4. Use a fork to seal the edges all around, and brush the top with beaten egg. Repeat with the remaining puff pastry, apple preserves, sliced apples, and egg.

5. Place the apple pies in the air fryer basket. Cook for 10 minutes, flipping half way, until the pastry is golden and puffed. Allow to cool before serving.

Tip: you can serve this dessert with fresh whipping cream, ice cream, caramel sauce, or chocolate sauce.

Made in the USA
Monee, IL
22 April 2022